THE TREE OF LIFE

TALKS BY
BUNTIE WILLS

First Published in Great Britain in 1990
by The Buntie Wills Foundation

This edition published in Great Britain in 2016
by Archive Publishing, Dorset, England

© 2016 Archive Publishing

A CIP Record for this book is available from
the British Cataloguing in Publication data office

ISBN 978-1-906289-32-4 (paperback)

All rights reserved.
No part of this publication may be reproduced, stored in a retrieval system, or transmitted at any time or by any means digital, electronic, mechanical, photocopying, recording or otherwise, without the prior written permission of the publisher.

www.archivepublishing.co.uk

www.transpersonalbooks.com

CONTENTS

Acknowledgements	i
Introduction	1
The method of approaching the papers	5

The papers
1	The Tree	13
2	The Kingdom	22
3	The Lower Self: Personality	30
4	The Higher Self: Individuality	37
5	The World of Spirit	49
6	Dynamism and Magnetism	57
7	Virtue and Vice	67
8	The Turning Point	76
9	Left Hand, Right Hand	83
10	The Poles	90

Histories
History of the Tree of Life	99
History of the Monday Group	102

Diagrams
The Triads and The Pillars	106
Glyph of the Tree of Life	107

ACKNOWLEDGEMENTS

This publication has been produced through the co-operative effort of the Books Group of the Buntie Wills Foundation. A companion volume, *Buntie Wills:Therapist – A Mosaic*, about her life and work, is also available from the Foundation.

Specific contributions to this book have been made by two members of the study group for whom the papers were originally written, Jean Simpson and Robert Smith; and also by Lois Graessle, Martin Robinson and Tina Robinson. Charles Chadwyck-Healey has given both advice and practical help with the printing. The Group is grateful to Geoff Green for designing the book, to Alison Moss for supervising the printing, and to Peter Miles and Tracey Ayre for computer support.

The members of the Books Group, which has overseen the project throughout, are Peggie Brown, Charles Chadwyck-Healey, Annie Elkins, Lois Graessle, Mildred Masheder, Vicki Mackenzie, Jean Simpson, Dee Purrett-Smith, Robert Smith and Carol Spero.

The Books Group volunteered to prepare this presentation in order to make Buntie's early spiritual teaching available to all members and friends of the Buntie Wills Foundation, in particular later pupils and those who did not have the opportunity to know her. To meet that aim we have kept as close as possible to the original writings, but a certain amount of editing and some new material have been felt necessary for clarity and accessibility. The random references to Indian teachings relate to previous work of the original study group and are not necessary to this text. They have been retained as useful correspondences for those familiar with the teachings. At times, however, these references may appear contrary to your own study of the Eastern systems. We have no explanation to offer.

In a work of this nature, necessarily dependent upon material derived from numerous sources, it is often difficult to ascertain whether or not particular information is in copyright. If we have unwittingly infringed copyright in any way, we tender our sincere apologies and will be glad of the opportunity to make appropriate acknowledgement in any future edition.

INTRODUCTION

As a member in the 1960s of a study group led by the psychotherapist Buntie Wills, I learned to value an ancient wisdom known as the Tree of Life, or Qabalah. Until then life had been a daily and often painful puzzle to me and, no matter how I approached it, one I got wrong all too often. Now at last I had found something which made sense of it. In the group I learned its method, and from then on it became a friend for life. Even during long periods when I have paid it no attention whatever, it continued to work in its own way within me, and to offer up insight and understanding from time to time quite unbidden. I always return to it.

I am no expert on the Tree, but I have lived with it subjectively for many years now, and I can vouch that it is indeed a great and true guide to living and how best it is done.

*

Because the Tree of Life is the widest possible system of knowledge, Buntie chose it as the ground plan on which we worked and she taught in our group. She based on it the very many talks or papers, all carefully written beforehand, that she gave in the 'Monday Group' over a number of years. They contain a great deal of knowing – and much heart.

It is the hope and intention of the trustees of the Buntie Wills Foundation to make further papers available for personal study in the course of time. This volume, containing the first ten talks, builds the concept of the Tree itself. The papers were designed as one year's study and are the key to subsequent papers and together they contain the essence of Buntie's teaching and experience.

In the talks Buntie was concerned with the development of no less than our spiritual life – getting in touch with it, nourishing it, extending the boundaries of our awareness into those realms and drawing new strength from them. In other words, growing the deepest and fullest life possible. For us, the Tree was a map with which we set out on a treasure hunt – a psychological journey, a living journey inward towards understanding.

*

We began by perusing the map, by memorising the diagram of the Tree and becoming familiar with its pattern. The Tree contains several lesser patterns which, laid on top of one another, comprise the whole symbol, just as, for instance, three other flags make up the Union Jack.

A symbol communicates something literally unthinkable, that is, which cannot be understood in terms of thought, our highest faculty, but can only be apprehended by *an experience of realization*. This is intuition – learning from within. The symbol acts as a catalyst to bring this about.

The Tree of Life symbol represents the great principles and laws of the universe, of creation – its energies, levels of existence, polarities, rhythm and balance. Once learned, it can be used as a background against which to see all aspects of life and relationship. It is the blueprint of Life itself, that vast power and energy. It shows us the anatomy of the cosmos, the macrocosm. Because we are made in that image – 'as above, so below' – here too is detailed the true nature of humanity, the microcosm – your own true, full, most marvellous and almost entirely unsuspected nature!

*

A truth learned then, which I have realized for myself repeatedly since, is that the path the Tree offers is unique. It is complete. All other such systems of knowledge or religion correspond to only a part of the Tree, large or small.

It is because it is truly comprehensive that the Tree of Life is the finest meditation symbol we have. This approach is open to you as soon as you are able to visualize the Tree fully at will. This visualization and contemplation of the material of each talk along with it, are the methods by which we worked in the Monday Group. I have come to understand that these two result in experiential Qabalah, a living experience of one's deep self. [Note: This is quite distinct from the better known 'magical' or ritual way of working with the Qabalah, although their aims are, or should be, the same – the application of esoteric principles to daily living.]

*

'May you live in interesting times,' is an old Chinese curse, not a blessing. The times we are living in now are the kind to which they were referring – uncertain, disruptive, difficult, even turbulent. Above all, highly confusing.

I think it is now widely recognised that this is how the times must be to bring about the profound changes at all levels of existence for which the world is now due with the evolution of a new age. But as individuals we still have to navigate our way through them, and for this we need all the help we can get.

Historically, whenever collective change is at a great peak in the world, as it is now, breaking down outworn patterns of understanding and belief, ancient wisdom emerges again in different forms to guide us at the levels we need to reach to be able to discern meaning.

In the 1960s Buntie Wills, as an intuitive, was certainly aware of its special value among those forms when she chose to work with the Tree of Life.

I remember her talking of the need of mankind for a minority of people who were capable of it to know and to hold to this kind of deep wisdom in times of great change for the human race – times such as she knew had already begun. These people would, she said, create and maintain a constant stable thread of consciousness throughout, and help to shape the future.

It is my belief that those of us who have taken up self discovery and growth, in the Foundation or in other ways, are already a part of this movement in our time, whether we realize it or not.

*

Thirty years ago Buntie Wills also saw, as many others have since, that C. G. Jung's depth psychology correlates perfectly with the Tree, and that the two were mutually enlightening. She based her talks on this relationship, in such a way that we have in them a much-needed and powerful bridge to the unconscious and a real guide to truth.

It is said that wisdom cannot be taught, only the way to it. The teachings gathered here offer such a way. They also offer education for new times.

Jean Simpson

THE METHOD OF APPROACHING THE PAPERS

Meditation

You will find a full illustration of the symbol of the Tree of Life on page 107. We would suggest that you photocopy it and use the copy as a 'bookmark' so that you can refer to it easily as you read this volume.

It will help you to make inner contact with the Tree if you colour in the spheres yourself on one or both copies: The Crown – silver; Wisdom – mother of pearl; Understanding – jet black; Mercy – blue; Severity – red; Beauty – yellow; Victory – green; Splendour – orange; The Foundation – purple; The Kingdom – top segment citrine, left-hand segment russet, right-hand segment olive-green, lower segment black.

At first sight, the Tree is a diagram – a pattern of circles linked together by straight lines. This is, however, a convenient two-dimensional representation, and for meditative purposes it should be seen as depicting a three-dimensional body, with the circles as full spheres and the whole rather like a mobile suspended in the air.

For meditation, visualize the Tree in your mind's eye against a background of total darkness. Think of a single stream of powerful energy welling up out of the darkness behind the topmost sphere, flowing into it and on down the pattern of the Tree from top to bottom in this order:

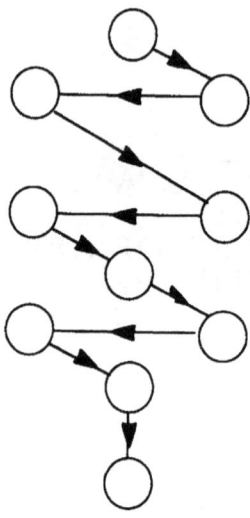

The energy pauses to vitalize each sphere and bring its colour to life, and then flows on through it. When the energy arrives at the lowest sphere, see the Tree complete, poised in perfect suspended balance, and think of the colours of the spheres as the light shining from them, contrasting with the darkness beyond.

Regarded in this way the pattern of the Tree reflects Wholeness, the essential unity of all things known and unknown to humanity.

The stream of energy is Spirit, pouring out of the Great Unmanifest, and creating different levels and centres, all manifestations of itself, the last of which is the 'place' in which Man has his roots.

When you know the Tree well enough to visualize the image in your mind accurately at will, without reference to the diagram, complete the process by thinking of yourself as connected with that lowest sphere, and then accepting the energy from it and taking it into yourself. You are then ready to continue with whatever meditation you wish.

At the end of a period of meditation, visualize the whole Tree just as you left it. Then return the energy from yourself to the lowest sphere, and think of it flowing back up the Tree in reverse order from bottom to top, and finally dwindling away into the darkness behind the top sphere.

*

Before reading any of the talks, create the image of the Tree in your mind as described above – or at least study the diagram for a few minutes. This is important for ordinary comprehension of the material, as well as for the inner working related to it. When you finish reading, 'close' the tree by returning the energy as above, or take a last look at the diagram.

*

Contemplation

A necessary condition of the process of working with the Tree of Life is that you read the talks with a truly open mind, and let the material flow into it unjudged. Do not expect to understand it immediately, or feel that you have failed in not doing so. If only two or three sentences 'come alive' for you, they are enough. The material is not designed primarily to convey information to you.

Instead the Tree of Life employs the language of symbol, which is rather enigmatic to us in the world today but was commonly familiar in ancient times. It is a potent language to do with the calling of images to your mind. Its effect is to touch you at certain levels and to wake in you the dormant faculty that can understand what the language conveys. It stimulates your own inner perception.

Try to read the material easily, giving the words your simple, full attention rather than approaching it as heavy, intensive study.

Once you have the Tree and the material in your mind, they will 'work' together there with only a little conscious effort on your part. Ponder them day to day, for whatever period of time you choose for the purpose. Simply let your thought and feeling play freely with what you have taken in.

Re-read the material occasionally if you can, and contemplate the ideas and the patterns contained in it. Consider the subject in relation to your ordinary living, and its relevance to you personally. Question what it means to you, and endeavour to recognize its principles in yourself and in the world about you.

Pieces of understanding, large or small, will come to you from time to time out of contemplation; on other occasions it will serve as a stepping stone on the way to them. You may experience recognition of a truth; or a knowing that you see something clearly; or a feeling of release when you suddenly understand something; or a sense of a barrier going down.

Do not underestimate these occurrences by thinking that you are understanding 'only' in your own way – that is the way you are looking for! However small or great, frequent or infrequent, these are all vital experiences, each leading to another. It is by these flashes of *en - light- enment* that you bring about your own growth.

*

Response

Just as the image on a photographic print needs 'fixing' in order to retain it, so any understanding you receive from living contemplation needs to be 'grounded' or its realization will be incomplete and it will be lost again instead of becoming a part of your knowing.

You ground it by giving it physical 'form and shape' of some kind by your own effort. This means expressing in an outward way your personal response to the material you have read. This is an activity which often adds enlightenment of its own.

It can be carried out in different ways. For instance –

1. You can write down what you have been caused to think and feel, or questions which have been raised within you, or perhaps what you have found for yourself. There is value in keeping any pieces you write all together in one folder, or writing them in a single notebook, for your eyes only.

2. You may envisage a drawing, a painting, or perhaps a model or sculpture which expresses something for you out of the talk. If so, make it. It does not matter if you are not an artist – this is not for showing to other people, but simply for your own inner purpose. The fact of its being made is important, not the end result.

3. You might make a geographical search for some representation of what the subject comes to mean to you, or undertake a 'pilgrimage' to where you know one exists.

4. If you have any dreams related to the talk, you can record them in whatever manner feels most comfortable or natural to you.

If you do this grounding too soon after your reading, it will probably represent only your *reaction* to the talk - what you immediately think or feel about it. *Response* is what you arrive at after going past that stage and then giving the matter longer and deeper consideration. You are likely to go through more than one level of 'seeing' something during the time you have allocated to the contemplation, rather like peeling away the layers of an onion and seeing ever deeper into it.

Try to have your inner intention clear when you start, so that your grounding is response, and not reaction.

The ten talks in this set were originally given at intervals spread over a period of a year, to be worked on step by step. It is strongly recommended that you follow this time pattern, spacing them out to suit your worldly commitments. It is also recommended that you do not read ahead, but meet each talk freshly at the time you appoint for it.

THE PAPERS

1

THE TREE

W.B. Yeats the poet, who was a keen follower of the Tree of Life in the late 1800s, once described it rather unpoetically as a geometric figure composed of spheres or circles joined by paths or straight lines. He also pointed out, a little more poetically, that in ancient times man saw it as a great natural tree, covered with foliage and fruits.

It was known in this way until a period, possibly around the 13th century, when knowledge of it was touched by the mathematical genius of Arabian thought, and the natural tree form was replaced by the two- or three-dimensional form we use today. Nevertheless we do well to recall the natural form from time to time, to remind us of the living-and-growing aspect of the Tree, the organic quality of the Life it represents.

The object of our work and study in these talks will be to use the geometrical form of the Tree to create a kind of mental filing system into which you can place as you gather it the very varied information and knowledge that you receive from the talks, reading and meditation. In this way we shall all be helped to give some sort of form and shape to those deeper glimpses that we all receive – through dreams, our work, and in therapy as well.

There is a Taoist myth which tells that:

'At the beginning of the no-beginning, Spirit and Matter met in mortal combat, until the Sun of Heaven triumphed over the Demon of Darkness – but not without damage to the Blue Dome of the Heavens. Out of the eastern se rose a Queen who, wielding the five-coloured Rainbow of Love in her magic cauldron, rebuilt the sky.'

We may not be aware of it, but each one of us needs to rebuild our sky of hope and peace. For our heaven in the West has been shattered in the struggle for wealth and power, and darkened by the Demon's shadow of egotism and vulgarity, knowledge bought with a 'bad conscience,' charity a word and deed for the sake of utility, a salve for the 'bad conscience.' As a result we are cut off from our original wholeness and the sense of it. We are held in the world of Matter, which is represented on the Tree diagram by the lowest sphere, named Malkuth, and we lack awareness of and connection to our true origin, Spirit, which is represented by the highest sphere, named Kether.

In short, we are in exile.

Yet each one of us carries within us, whether we know it or not, the power, the desire, the longing, to 'rebuild our sky' – that is, to find a way of transformation so that we can feel whole and know we are fully a part of Creation, as was intended for us at the dawn of humanity. If we get in touch with this inherent longing, hidden deep in our unconscious, we will awaken the power it contains, which is always there waiting to bring about our wholeness. It will act on us in such a way that we are gradually transformed.

This transformation must begin within the earth level of consciousness, where we must remain rooted. (Those of you who have studied the Indian systems will understand this as the awakening and opening of the muladhara or lowest chakra.) At the centre of our earthly being, which is the cauldron of alchemy, the energy awoken influences as the fire works on the contents of the cauldron: it does not destroy, but transmutes. Its power is concerned only with the 'way home' to wholeness, whereby the divine spiritual essence which dwells in each one of us is freed from entanglement with matter and form, not to become separate from it, but to govern it from a higher level. There, our higher self is capable of resisting evil in all its forms, and disintegration, which both constantly threaten the lower, material body.

If, however, we try to ignore the earth level of being, to avoid the regions where the entanglement holds us and progress before we have made good preparation there, then we cut ourselves off from our own roots and the growth we make will be poor and unsupported.

We need those roots, our full instinctual life set deep in the centre of our earth. They need to be cleansed and refreshed, so that they can stabilize the tree which is each one of us, and bring to it the nourishment needed to grow the stem and branches so that they can blossom and bear fruit in full maturity.

Many spiritual teachers have pointed out that if we try to escape the discipline of matter before we have mastered its lessons, the deep life energy does not lend us its impetus but remains hidden in the depths, and we find our tree has no strength. At that point we tend to rush to all sorts of uplift books and uplift organizations, hoping to find a quick cure for all our ills. It is not difficult to see that they too become merely a way of escape and certainly not a way of advancement. Others who cannot face life at the earth level dissociate from it and fall into psychological sickness.

This withering of the Tree of Life in man is because he is distracted from himself and out of touch with the basis of his being. The real need is for a creative pause or period in our life given over to regaining this lost sense of origin, of rhythm, continuity and balance, so that we can begin again to feel the sap rise.

Part of the distraction from which we suffer is intellectual distraction and indigestion from reading too many books, the contents of which disappear into the wrong channels. This work on the Tree of Life will set up right channels to special places in your mind which you can fill with good material, and where you can maintain some form of clarity and discrimination, instead of becoming muddled and confused in every direction with too many words and ideas.

*

The universe is founded on order, and we ourselves reflect that order. Those of you who have been studying Raja Yoga have come to understand that the human mind functions in three different states. The first of these is darkness, and it acts only to injure: no other idea comes into that state of mind. The second state is an active state whose chief motives are power and enjoyment. In the third state the mind is in a condition of serene calm.

Psychologically speaking 'hell' – as for example when we say 'I have been through hell,' or 'I am going through hell' – is the absorption of the soul into its own darkness. Nevertheless even if phantasms created by human passions do plunge the self into hell, the human being can only feel its torments insofar as the image of God has not been completely dimmed. C.G.Jung has said that in itself hell is illusory, but it may nevertheless be the greatest psychological subjective reality for the individual. Effective struggle against hell, which is a state of mind, consists entirely in awakening the spiritual life. Lack of sufficient spiritual life and development in the individual necessarily gives rise to evil dreams and nightmares and other dark states. Hell is the inability to love, and is an isolation from and also an enslavement by everything and everyone. It is feeling lost, abandoned, a complete separation from the divine source. It is thus that we are held by our own Demon of Darkness.

In early Christian times it was more or less assumed that everyone had a demon beyond their personal control, and the prevalent idea was that good and bad alike proceeded at different times from the demon of each individual. One's demon would be recognised as being powerful and benevolent at one time, and weak and malevolent at another. The gradual differentiation between the beneficent and the malignant qualities of demons resulted eventually in acceptance of their division for each one of us into a good spirit or guardian angel (a clear mirror for God), and an evil spirit or devil (a distorting mirror which was employed in frustrating the good purposes of God).

In time the evil devils came to be seen as marshalled under one spirit or devil proper, the supreme impersonation of the spirit of evil who came to represent them all, namely Satan. Everything he touches is corrupted, everything good and worthwhile withers, every aspiration is tainted and cheapened. But because he is incapable of grasping the true nature of that which is good he must therefore fail in the end.

The guardian angels come out in such conceptions as the famous good demon of Socrates, the 'noble, courageous and highly unmatchable spirit' which protected Shakespeare's Anthony, and Kipling's 'demon who is in charge' who was to be awaited and obeyed.

Even today we say to someone, 'Be an angel, or 'You're an absolute devil,' or 'Don't be a fiend.' This division into good spirits or angels, and evil spirits or devils within us is the first significant intimation in our psychology of the ambiguous function of our unconscious, seemingly involuntary to us, as both devourer and destroyer, and preserver and inspirer. It is found in a great variety of mythic forms in the past, which today express themselves in our dreams.

In one of these mythic forms, which appears in both legend and fairy stories, the hero deliberately swims or steers his boat into the jaws of the monster, cuts out the monster's heart with his sword, and eats it to satisfy his hunger. He then hews his way out of the monster's belly and not only saves himself but all the rest of his neighbours and relatives previously swallowed by the monster. This partaking of the demonic power, this swallowing of the power of the demon, is the very source of the hero's superhuman efficacy in destroying him. And it is by virtue of the heroic deed, after swallowing the demonic power, that he converts it into the Divine Power. It is the hero himself who forms the bridge or resolution between the two opposing powers, and brings them into relationship.

It is, incidentally, characteristic of a hero that his facing the demonic power results not only in his own freedom, but also in that of others. It is in this same pattern that Christ conquered death and hell and released the tormented spirits from prison.

Future talks will describe further different pairs of opposites involving our guardian angel and our dark demon, which constantly pull us in two directions. Broadly, these are:

	Related sphere
Discrimination/Inertia	**Malkuth**
Independence/Idleness	**Yesod**
Truthfulness/Dishonesty	**Hod**
Unselfishness/Unchastity	**Netzach**
Devotion/Pride	**Tiphareth**
Courage/Cruelty	**Geburah**
Obedience/Tyranny	**Chesed**
Silence/Avarice	**Binah**
Devotion (no opposition)	**Chokmah**
Attainment (no opposition)	**Kether**

You will also hear more about the Celestial Dragon or Serpent of Wisdom who twines about the Tree of Life – and is quite distinct from the Arch Tempter associated with the Tree of Knowledge. This serpent of wisdom corresponds with the Kundalini or Shakti Goddess below the muladhara chakra, and the Queen in the depths of the eastern sea. We will be using terms like this because all language relating to different states of existence, forces and processes is necessarily metaphorical and must make use of images. From this we can understand that the image of the Tree of Life itself represents at one and the same time both macrocosm and microcosm, in that it symbolises the original emanative process of the universe, producing hells, earths and heavens. which also reflects itself in the psychological constitution of the human being.

The biologist Sir Julian Huxley in his introduction to The *Phenomenon of Man* by the theologian Father Teilhard de Chardin (which, by the way, is essentially concerned with the Tree of Life), says 'We, mankind, contain the possibilities of the earth's immense future, and can real-ize more and more of them on condition that we increase our knowledge and our love.'

Many people over the centuries have been perplexed about what they saw as the problem of evil, of that which is not good spirit. More recent thinkers have asked not, 'Why should evil exist?' but 'Why should the Absolute change in this world into some lesser thing?' The Qabalah recognises that the original process of manifestation necessarily includes potential evil and they cannot be separated; also that there are laws which govern when evil becomes more than merely potential.

*

The doctrine of the Qabalah is that:

– it is by number (order) and sound (vibration) that the universe takes form,
– the Tree is the pattern of the process of this cosmic form-taking,
– the Tree is a diagram of manifested existence.

You will discover that in the Qabalah this manifested existence is shown to be divided into four planes of existence: They are, from the top of the Tree to the bottom:

1. The Archetypal (Atziluth) – the top upward-pointing triad of spheres on the diagram: *Kether, Chokmah, Binah*

2. The Creative (Briah) – the next, downward-pointing triad of spheres: *Geburah, Chesed, Tiphareth*

3. The Formative (Yetzirah) – the third, down-pointing triad of *Hod, Netzach, Yesod*

4. The Material (Assiah) – the sphere of *Malkuth*

The energy which emanates projects downwards downwards through all four planes, and each plane can be represented by a full tree. These levels, or spheres of influence, are those through which Beatrice guided Dante in the *Paradiso*. There are definite indications that Dante knew the Qabalah teaching, and indeed the order of his Paradisal spheres certainly agrees with that of the Tree of Life.

On entering the heaven of the fixed stare, Beatrice tells Dante:

'Here is the gold, whence motion in his race
Starts: Motionless the centre, and the rest
   All move around . . .
The vase wherein time's roots are plunged thou seest:
Look elsewhere for the leaves . . . .'

The Qabalah Tree is the key to all religious systems, and the great art of secret relationships, for example, in geometry, between each figure and its symbol; in astrology, between the planets, metal, colours, plants, animals; in alphabets, between the letter and the word.

The philosopher Rene Schweble in his *Problem of Evil* wrote, 'The Word does not express an idea, it creates it.' One could say that the whole of ritual is based on the power of the word.

'In the Beginning (in the first principle) was the Word, and the Word was God (and with God).' The power of the Word is the power which connects by an invisible thread everything which exists: the all-pervading power, the power of the Word and of Number.

2

THE KINGDOM

The Tree of Life sets out for us a study in *relationship*.

The prime relationship shown is that between Spirit (Kether, at the top of the Tree) and Matter (Malkuth, at the bottom of the Tree). We often refer to these two as 'living' spirit and 'dead' matter, but this is inaccurate: matter is inert, but it is not dead. That is why we cannot simply turn away from the world of matter, rejecting it as being too difficult for us, or too mundane, or mere distraction from higher things. Every attempt to escape from its natural discipline and due influence in our everyday existence is a regression psychologically, and exceedingly harmful to the psyche.

We are children of the material plane, born of the earth, and if we want to achieve our own wholeness it is our first task to set about coming into good relationship with it. It has much to reveal to us if we learn to see it in a new way: we need to discover that it is, in fact, friendly to us and not, as so many believe, in opposition. It offers us great opportunity. To the extent that we open our minds and change our attitude to the world of matter, learning to understand its true nature, so we free ourselves to relate to it positively and are no longer locked in its inertia. Here is the starting point of transformative growth. But matter cannot be understood in its own terms alone.

*

Pure spirit (Kether) is absolute, unconditional and abstract. Matter, the earth level (Malkuth) is relative, conditional, and concrete.

Extreme idealists try to realize the absolute without the relative. Extreme materialists try to realize the relative without the absolute. On the one hand this is like trying to realize the concept of an 'inside' without the accompanying one of an outside; on the other hand it is trying to realize an 'outside' without an inside. They can only be understood in relation to each other.

Pure Spirit, which lies beyond the limitations of time and space, is a state of existence, a kind of intelligence capable of knowing itself, or an energy. Matter is contained within both time and space, but it too is a state, intelligence or energy.

In the beginning Spirit (Kether) issued forth and emanated several intermediary stages (the intervening spheres), evolving through each as a different state of being – just as a river flowing from the mountains to the sea changes its character completely in different types of terrain on the way, but remains the very same water. In this way Spirit emerged finally in a state of concrete form – Matter – which is dense but also very much alive, an active energy. The nuclear age has brought into everyday knowledge what the esoteric world has long known.

If we realize that all visible things have their origin in Spirit, then the whole of creation is seen to be the Spirit's 'modus operandi,' in expressing itself, culminating in the world of Matter. But creation, like the river, continues perpetually to flow and there is a constant outpouring of the Spirit which, having fulfilled itself in the creation of Matter, must then begin to return whence it came, completing a cycle. Malkuth, the outermost point, is the nadir.

All this is true not only of the cosmos, but also of each one of us. Here in the earth level to which we are born is the turning point where evolution begins for the cosmos and for us. (Darwin's biological evolution is only a very tiny part of this great impulse.) We ourselves are part of the world of Malkuth and it is here in ourselves as we naturally are, in our ordinary world, the moving panorama of people and events coming and going, the rise and fall of nations and people, that the life energy we call Spirit has to come to fruition and begin the return. Most of us are unaware that we live in that current and have its impulse within us.

All the work of the universe consists in the *material-ization* of spirit or the *spirit-ualization* of matter, and we are concerned with both.

*

You can see from the diagram that Malkuth is not quite like the other spheres. It is more complicated, containing a pattern of its own. This is because it is not only the ultimate expression of its polar opposite Kether, but also includes expression of each of the individual intervening spheres or emanations. Malkuth is the embodiment of form, and all things are present in its form and are visible there to those who attain in-sight – who learn to see into the density of matter, which otherwise veils the emanations contained there so that they are but 'seen through a glass darkly.'

It is from Yesod, the sphere immediately above it, that Malkuth receives emanation of the energies or forces gathered there from the down-flowing energy. In Yesod they have nebulous, psychic form: the energy is 'such stuff as dreams are made of' until it begins to transform and 'body forth' the material particles of Malkuth. The material plane of Malkuth is the outward and visible evidence of the invisible forms of Yesod, just as a chair is the visible evidence resulting from the idea of sitting, the concept of a chair, and its design.

In Malkuth, energy exists in four conditions: Earth, Fire, Air and Water. (These are not the chemical elements with which we are familiar, although they include them, but are higher equivalents, and we will distinguish them by initial capitals.) The sphere of Malkuth is the form and coherence of these four parts, which are held together by inertia.

We all know from experience the large amount of energy we need in order to move physical matter, its inertia being experienced by us as heaviness, and having to be overcome. Similarly we too are held by inertia, which makes us tend to continue living just as we find ourselves, even though we do not like our condition, rather than raise the energy to overcome this tendency and begin to change.

Inertia is by nature resistant and unresponsive to change, but it can be worked on through the power of one of the elements – Fire. To begin our transformational change we need to obtain a response from our own Fire. We need to warm to our hope and aim, and to energize our natural state with the vitalizing spark of enthusiasm – be it interest, curiosity, or simply puzzlement. We talk of being 'fired with' something. It empowers us. It quickens our bodily system and overrides inertia. It opens the mind to possibility, and trying to envision that possibility. It is by this envisioning, the quality of Yesod itself, that we are able to approach the other elements in matter and examine in new light the forms manifested around us. What we see in the earth level cannot be understood in terms of that plane, but only by the forces which brought it into being.

We can also speak of these forces and forms in terms of mankind, psychological terms, as though they were conscious and purposeful. In so doing we acknowledge the intelligence of the subtler forces, while stopping short of personifying them. It is our own intelligence which will help us to discriminate between what is important and what is unimportant, to sacrifice the unreal for the real, to expand in consciousness and to facilitate the gradual absorption of the lower into the higher.

We generally measure the 'livingness' of any individual life by its intelligence. The supreme principle of Light is the ultimate intelligence. Our personal evolution must be through our increasing awareness of this universal principle and our own individual relation to it, resulting in all our actions, inner or outer, being in accordance with it. The eternal realities are brought together by God and form everything experienced in the universe. It is the Lord who is, though Himself unmoved, the First Mover in all things.

The individual's sense of this 'all-pervading Power' and his consciousness of it, is based on his subjective experience and is Truth for him however much others may refuse to accept such experience as Truth for themselves. Spiritual knowledge is not capable of verification or refutation – this is possible only for sensory knowledge. Our own Truth also provides us with a proper source for all our actions. The power and our awareness of it are twin aspects of the same intelligence. It is with our highest consciousness that we realize this fully - the inner self in its being-consciousness, the intelligence which is therefore the sole basis of reality and of action in our world of Malkuth. Until we realize that, we identify our consciousness with the seeming duality of Spirit and Matter. When we reach the realization we cease to identify and are being-conscious. We then carry out our worldly duties and actions unaffected by any sense of separate identity and at peace within, and the results are in harmony with the all-pervading power. This is the true concept of efficiency, which is a quality discovered not outside but *within* us – and transcendental support is implicit in it.

The ancient Greeks are a perfect example of this efficiency. They clearly understood the necessity that in order to achieve a perfection of form, there must be a perfection of function. It gave them their great sensitivity to perfection in both cases, and resulted in their way of life and the creation of so much that was timelessly full of beauty. They knew that matter was not to be seen as some ultimate depth of unspirituality, and they embraced it. We need to learn what they understood. Malkuth is a necessary lesson before we can begin to aspire heavenwards.

*

The highest degree of self-recognition is that which realises its own spiritual nature. To live in the mode of the relative is to be subject to conditions; to live in the truth of the absolute is to govern conditions.

Conceiving of pure Spirit as the underlying origin of all things is to recognize the innermost nature of all being and that it is limitless. No matter where Spirit is found to exist, it is *totally* present – this is its own law.

When Jung speaks of the collective unconscious, he is also recognizing this all-pervading, intelligent Spirit as universally subjective mind. It permeates all space and all matter. It is the creative power throughout nature. Wherever we find creative power at work we are in the presence of subjective mind, whether on the grand scale of the cosmos, or the smaller but comparable scale of the individual.

Today there is a growing realization in all of us of the link between the science of matter and phenomena, and the psychic or inner pattern of all things. Science no longer adheres solely to a materialistic explanation of life. Psychotherapy now recognizes that similar results do not always spring from similar causes in the realms of the mind, but that temperament intervenes. The fourfold pattern of Malkuth already seen in the Elements is reflected also in the four types of human temperament. Each of these represents three contained within it, making twelve in all, which are themselves reflected in the signs of the Zodiac:

Earth – phlegmatic temperament:
those born under Taurus, Virgo, Capricorn

Water – melancholic temperament:
those born under Cancer, Scorpio, Pisces

Air – sanguine temperament:
those born under Libra, Gemini, Aquarius

Fire – choleric temperament:
those born under Aries, Sagittarius, Leo

Whatever our temperaments, as our consciousness of the unity between these four Elements linked by one eternal life, becomes more refined so the Spirit as source of life becomes more apparent to us.

The things that a person of the world considers valuable are cast aside by the more spiritual person. He or she will become increasingly aware that the universe exists for the sake of the Self; that the powers of the Self can manifest through the matter that envelops them. The whole of evolution is one in essence, the sequence the same, all the laws one, however different in their stages of manifestations. The Self in you is the same as the universal Self. Whatever powers manifest themselves throughout the world, those same powers exist, in latency, in you.

*

If the outer world wearies you, how do you expect to conquer the difficulties of the inner? We are tempered ready for the task by meeting all the little troubles of our everyday world and relationships. Running away and avoiding our personal problems means spiritual regression and negativity, and lost opportunity.

If we harden the heart and become intellectual and cold towards our personal world, perhaps even turning our backs on family ties, we only put a barrier round the Self, who is the Kingdom, the Power and Glory. We isolate ourselves by it, just when we need to embrace others. If we harden the heart when we need to do all we can to soften and sensitize it, we kill off love – the very thing which links us, at one and the same time, to each other and the Whole. Take it on yourself to suffer from it and for it rather than reject it. Pain passes away, but the love continues to grow and is the great attracting force which makes all things one.

Do not, in trying to be super-human, become sub-human. It is by and through human ties of love, understanding and sympathy that the Self unfolds. We must try to become what we are: to become in outer manifestation that which we are in inner reality. Psychologically speaking, we must become uninhibited and manifest this intelligence whatever the condition of the material vehicle. The only way you can know God is by diving into yourself, turning within. Then you will find Him and know that He is without as well as within you, in the world and at your centre.

The Upanishad tells you that in the quietude of the mind and in the tranquillity of the senses, a man may behold the majesty of the Self.

3

THE LOWER SELF: PERSONALITY

It is an important step when we realise that while we have our existence in the world of Matter we have it in three other 'worlds' at the same time. They are the worlds of Emotion, of Mind and of Spirit. They represent a large portion of our being, and yet we are for the most part unconscious of them.

They are seen as horizontal divisions on the Tree, and each world is identified by a group of three spheres, as against the single sphere of the world of Matter, Malkuth. It is the interaction of the energies of the three spheres which creates the 'field of existence' or world. (See page 106, top diagram.)

For us as microcosm of the great pattern of creation, Malkuth represents the tangible external world of physical matter, and our ordinary sensory and brain consciousness of it with its attachment to objects, object-bound ideas, and extravert materialism.

As soon as we become conscious of Yesod, we stand at the gateway of the primary world behind the objects. The astral or emotional world (seen as the triad of spheres Yesod, Hod and Netzach) has great importance for us because through it we make contact with the transcendental world. It is one of the great achievements of modern psychology that it has demonstrated this, so vindicating the role of feeling in our lives, and demonstrating that it has primacy over reason for us.

The emotional world is the invisible one of images and fantasies, our area of inner subjective reaction to the ordinary world about us. It is our unconscious emotional life, or in Jungian terms our personal unconscious.

Most of us have real fear of any light thrown into this dark corner, as it is chaotic and contains a great deal that we are afraid to admit to ourselves, let alone to anyone else. But we need to clear this surface pattern, and unless we go into the personal unconscious carefully and examine our subjective fancies fully, we will never be able to reach the inner worlds of Mind and Spirit.

If we discover and work with our inner images, they will act as stepping stones for us in the chaos and we will be able to search our psychic and emotional feelings, changing the meaning of our past and creating new attitudes to live by. Gradually our imaginative faculty will become free, and instead of binding us to unconscious emotional motives, it will work for our greater good – for it is the key to contact with our deep inner self (Tiphareth on the Tree) and the worlds beyond it.

For the two lower worlds on the Tree comprise our Lower Self or Personality, the subjective unit of incarnation with its purely personal contents, conscious and unconscious. But when we become aware of our Tiphareth we are in touch with our Individuality or Higher Self.

While we may change the substance of our material and emotional bodies in our lifetime, our Higher Self, the Holy Guardian Angel assigned to each of us at birth, accompanies us until death. It is this Self which developed first in us originally, around the Divine Spark or nucleus of the soul, the Spirit level of our being.

*

The outward observation of surface psychology and the interpretation of psychological activity are purposeless, because they are limited to the materialistic viewpoint. We cannot explain either mind or matter in terms of themselves alone. We cannot explain mind without employing terms of the senses, or living matter without employing terms of consciousness. It is not the form which confines the life, but the life that determines the form. That is why to understand Malkuth it must be approached through Yesod, the receptive chalice which gathers together the down-flowing forces of the Tree; and Yesod can only be understood by approaching it through the meaning of Hod, where the forces received are designed before emanation to Yesod; and the approach to Hod is through Netzach, the centre of instinctual emotion. The universe is therefore insoluble to the materialist because he insists on trying to explain it in terms of his own as a material universe – an impossible situation as nothing can be explained in terms of itself, but only in relation to a higher power, or a greater whole.

*

In the Lower Self, Netzach corresponds with the dynamic animal nature of the soul, the urge to life, and the free-moving natural forces flowing from it are constrained by the rational mind in the sphere of Hod, who directs them to ends that are willed and designed. Direction or control is naturally at the expense of fluidity and operates through the use of symbols and formulae in order to prevent diffusion. Hod is essentially the sphere in which the forces of nature and Spirit take on sensible form. It is the sphere where our capacities for reaction are lifted out of the sphere of emotional reflexes and brought under rational control.

We need to respond to Netzach and feel our own deep instinctual emotion, but at the same time we need to have the capacity of Hod to restrain or refrain at will from this response, in order not to become dependent on the sphere of Netzach but become a true initiate of it.

A cold-blooded individual of rational and dominating will cannot become an initiate; neither can an overly-sentimental, overly-fluid and emotional individual. There must be a link between our power of imaginative sympathy and the power of concentrated will to live fully and wisely on the plane of Malkuth.

The initiation ceremony was once an outward pattern of ritual revealing the mysteries, but it is now *the making conscious of what was previously unconscious*. Allowing our unconscious patterns to respond blindly to various stimuli produces uncontrolled reactions. By making these unconscious patterns conscious, we can bring them under the control of the will and the higher Self, our higher intelligence. Where a solid concreted 'pavement' has been built up by Hod over the unconscious, the problem is less that of reaction as in Netzach, but increasingly that of inaction.

The average human intellect works through a connection between Hod and Malkuth, and this is the pattern of the logical-minded person. It is in Hod, the concrete intellect, that the personal human mind begins to function. It is also the realm of the scientist. Netzach, its opposite, is the realm of artists, and the free-moving shifting collective pattern of instincts. Yesod is quite simply the unconscious, filled with ancient and forgotten things repressed since the childhood of the race. Hod contains the keys that will unlock the doors of Yesod's treasure house. But like all things in nature Hod, unfertilized by its opposite polarity, is sterile and produces all theory and no practice. It is through the Netzach in our own nature that the elemental, instinctual forces obtain access to consciousness; until Netzach is in function for us they remain in the unconscious sphere of Yesod, working blindly.

*

In the functioning of the emotional triad we are able to draw at personal level on the two great spiritual powers of *generation* which created the universe: the great original Activity and Passivity seen high on the Tree as Chokmah, called Abba the Father, and Binah, the Great Mother. We make contact with them in our personal image-world as symbols, and they make accessible to us our own *regeneration*.

They are eternally symbolized by the phallus and the bowl. We find them in primitive rites as the fire-stick and the cup in which it bores; in Roman times as the fundus in the earth in the centre of the camp into which each soldier threw his spear. Then there is the chalice of the Holy Grail into which a spear, perpetually dripping blood, was thrust, and the holy font of baptism, fertilized by plunging in the lighted candle.

The spiritual meaningfulness of these symbols can never be exhausted. They recur again and again, and we can only hope to understand them to the extent to which we have made their meaning our own through the spiritual experience of regeneration or rebirth. It is through this process and our taking part in it that the truth is 'shown forth' in the world through us, and through it those who can understand may partake in a new life which should be ever renewed, like the life of the ancient and eternal Moon. We cannot repeat the pattern of renewal too often.

When by spiritual regeneration we bring the highest spiritual forces into the world of Matter, the Divine Man so easily thought of as partaking of the upper planes then stands with his feet firmly planted on Mother Earth (or if seated Eastern-fashion the anus corresponds) and the generative organs relate to Yesod. These lower levels are also divine; nothing that emanates from God is unclean unless we allow it to become so. If we evade and avoid this fact, how are we to keep ourselves clean and wholesome? Hence the expression 'cleanliness is next to godliness' – especially inward cleanliness.

It is through discrimination in Malkuth that we learn rejection of the excreta of life inwardly, and many of our decisions would be made easier if we bore this in mind. Practising discrimination will also teach us the need for letting go or giving up in order to obtain that which is greater. In this way we can rise out of our limitations and our over-retentiveness or avarice, which produce mere waste or excreta. The uniting of the higher Self with the lower self happens through the complete absorption of the lower by the higher. This is what is meant by the way of the initiate. The womb of Mother Earth is the gate to the spiritual life. The Greater Mother, Binah, is the origin of form and of Mother Earth, the sphere of form.

Wherever there is organised form there is the life force, for life alone is the organiser. Malkuth is inanimate matter until or unless the powers of Yesod ensoul it – and this is a marriage between the masculine and feminine. All such union is a sacrament, a sacrament being an outward and visible sign of an inward and spiritual grace.

The moon and the generative organs are both symbols of Yesod. The rhythm of the feminine is to be found in the rhythmical nature of the moon. And in Yesod we meet the dual symbolism of male and female force and form: the Moon, Yesod, and the Earth, Malkuth, which share one etheric double. All etheric activities are at their most active when the moon is full. During the dark phases of the moon, etheric energy is at its lowest and all unorganized forces have a tendency to rise up and give trouble as the life forces are relatively weak and the unbalanced forces are relatively strong. Hence a troubled person is called 'luna-tic.'

But the Moon is said to have a tree of her own which is the source of inspiration and wisdom; it is sacred and bears the fruit of knowledge and understanding. By asking an oracle from her, and through the images and symbols she offers as reply, we can gain the fruit. The fruit of the Tree of Life (of which the Moon and her tree are a part) is the immortality of free spirit.

*

All life contains a varying degree of psychic or Yesodic activity, and every psychic process is an image and an imagination, otherwise no consciousness could exist. In Western mysticism we are told how through knowledge of our own nature we may rise above personality and attain the inner and God-like man. The 14th century Flemish mystic John of Ruysbroeck makes use of an image also known in Indian philosophy and in Nordic myth – that of the Tree whose roots are above (Kether, root of Air; Binah, root of Water; Chokmah, root of Fire) and its branches below: 'And he must climb up into the Tree of Faith, which grows from above downwards for its roots are in the Godhead.'

It is in this that the unity of being consists, and this means 'being turned inwards' – a man turned within, into his own heart, that he may understand and feel the inner working and the inner words of God. This new state of consciousness born of religious practice (in the broadest sense) is distinguished by the fact that no longer do outward things affect an ego-bound consciousness.

'It is no longer I who live, but Christ who lives in me.'

4

THE HIGHER SELF: INDIVIDUALITY

When we first discover our own innate urge to ascend out of what we already are to higher being, there is a tendency to remove ourselves from others in order to do it, as though we must avoid their influence to be able to find our true self. But this is a retrograde step initiated by the ego, which is always concerned with separateness. It is naturally excited at the new prospect but, as Pierre Teilhard de Chardin pointed out, its mistake – and a fatal one – is to confuse personality, where the ego has true place, with individuality, where it does not. The way to full realization of ourselves as individuals is through what links us with others at a deep level, for it is there that the individual qualities of our nature become defined.

Those forced to share a crucial or life-threatening situation where the ego, centre of the personality, becomes powerless, soon recognize how much they have in common meeting totally as human beings, and through that each one discovers just what it is that makes him truly individual. This is equally true where the meeting in depth is positive, i.e. voluntarily undertaken.

A crab might resent being described only as 'a crustacean', but it is when he realizes that he is a crustacean that he discovers what it is that makes him a crab among them.

*

It is not until we enter into contact with Tiphareth on the Tree that we are in touch with our individuality. There we meet a resonance in ourselves which opens the gateway to the archetypal world of deep collective experiencing, represented by the triad of spheres Tiphareth, Geburah and Chesed. (See top diagram on page 106).

The highest plane of being, the world of Spirit (Kether-Chokmah-Binah) is for all practical purposes beyond our comprehension. But it includes certain principles which need to be recognised: the fundamental principles of Activity or Force (Chokmah, the Father) and Passivity or Form (Binah, the Great Mother), and creating these the Source of All (Kether). These principles and their interaction generate manifestation, and this triad represents for us latent Spirit, all-powerful potential.

As the power of this World of Spirit flows out of its own triad and down the Tree, the manifestation of that Spirit begins in the archetypal triad or World of Mind. This is not to be confused with the human intellect, which is generally related to Hod, but is defined as 'mind-stuff' or free-moving abstract mind, the first material of manifestation. It is here that as human beings we can meet the latent and transforming power of Spirit – when we have developed the awareness capable of it by clearing the way to it. And in this way we bring that awareness to our deep unconscious pattern. When we do our state is no longer personal, but supra-personal.

*

In Tiphareth there is synthesis of the consciousness of the lower and higher selves. It is the equivalent of what Pierre Teilhard de Chardin calls the 'Omega Point' where man is fulfilled, and individualised or integrated, by 'becoming lost in the Greater than himself. Spiritual synthesis means that in every organized whole, the parts perfect themselves and fulfil themselves. The more 'Other' they become in conjunction, the more they find themselves as 'Self'. 'By the structure,' Pere Teilhard de Chardin goes on to say, 'Omega, in its ultimate principle, can only be a distinct centre radiating at the core of a system of centres.

In his thinking the *affinity of being with being* – the true definition of love – is a general property of all life and of all the forms successively adopted by organized matter. Driven by the forces of love, the fragments of the world seek each other so that the world may come into being. Universal love is not only psychologically possible, it is the only complete and final way in which we are able to love.

Continuing, Pere Teilhard de Chardin urges us to overcome our 'anti-personalist' complex which paralyzes us, and to make up our minds to accept the possibility, indeed the reality, of some *source* of love and *object* of love at the summit of the world above our heads. If the universe ahead of us assumes a face and a heart, and personifies itself, so to speak, then in the atmosphere of this focus the elemental attraction will immediately blossom. In the centre, so glaring as to be disconcerting, is the uncompromising affirmation of a personal God. In one sense the Kingdom of God is a big family. In another it is a prodigious biological operation, that of the redeeming incarnation. Christ born as a man among men inserted himself into the general ascent of consciousness in order to purify, direct and superanimate it. By a perennial act of communion and sublimation he aggregates to himself the total psyche of the earth, Malkuth. Christ as 'Omega Point' is the sun striking through the clouds of ignorance and unconsciousness; one ray of it reflects on to that which is ascending that which is already on high – and is the rupture of our solitude.

*

All gods of healing are sun gods, and sunlight is the basis of the life process and of physical well-being. Indeed it is together the giver of life and the source of all being, as the Sun behind the sun is God the Father himself. Tiphareth is therefore the mediator through which we receive both physical and spiritual vitality, both consciously and unconsciously. It is the basis of all energy. Gold, the symbol of the sun, is the symbol of human energy in terms of money or wealth, which flows in and out according to the capacity of individuals. Physically these solar influences have their correspondence in the solar plexus, and all stresses and strains in connection with work and finance will cause trouble in that region. To be cut off from this solar energy or spiritual aspect of nature is due to our wrong mental attitude. By our refusal to acknowledge the 'naturalness' of our physical and spiritual well-being, our part in nature and nature's part in us, we create what we call 'inhibitions'; we inhibit this free flow of life-giving magnetism between the part and the whole. It follows that psychic and physical health is then impossible.

The lack of recognition on our part of the Giver of Life and of these higher aspects of nature can bring about an entirely false religious attitude. False refinements of the intellect which spur the more primitive sides of our own nature bring about dissociations and sexual repression that result in mental illness and psychic and spiritual diseases. Neuroses are the direct result of false values, false ideals, and of a false personality development.

Through the artificial conditions of life in the big cities, all manner of irrational taboos have grown up. The concrete pavement has cut us off inwardly and outwardly from our contact with the earth and our roots in nature, consequently breaking the natural circuit and our contact with the heavenly archetypes and cosmic currents. Dr. Albert Schweitzer's 'reverence for life' simply means the reverence we should give to natural manifestations of all spiritual processes. Constantly to insulate and inhibit their natural expression on the earth is to bring about chaos in the psyche.

The meaning of the word Tiphareth is Beauty, and Tiphareth's vision is of the harmony of natural things. Through Tiphareth we find the archetypal ideas which form the invisible framework of the whole of manifested natural creation. In this invisible anatomy Tiphareth is the breast, composed of the lungs, the heart and the great network of nerves known as the solar plexus.

Spiritually the heart is often known as 'the cave of the heart, which in Russian icons is the place of birth of the Divine Child. As mediator this Divine Child is the 'translator through sacrifice' of force or energy locked up in the form of Malkuth, freeing the force and circulating it again in the cosmos. This is what we mean when we speak of 'freedom of the spirit': it is the sacrifice of the static forms that imprison spiritual energy, freeing it into a higher state of consciousness.

The resonance through devotion or the chanting or uttering of the Sacred Name brings us into the right focussing of our attention and response to the power of the Name. It is vital for the initiate to have come to a full realization of the ultimate spiritual nature of all natural forces before he can handle them in their subjective form. All subjective emotions in our natures can only become servants of the higher Self when directed by the spiritual principles behind all life.

*

Tiphareth is the Christ-centre. It is:
1. *The centre of equilibrium* of the whole Tree of Life.
2. *The point of transmutation* between the planes of form and the planes of force – this transmutation of force being expressed as a sacrifice to God and act of sacrificial love.

3. *The connecting link* between the Archetypal Kingdom or Higher Self and the Kingdom of Form or Lower Self. In it we find seership, the higher psychism of the individual.

4. *The centre of transition* from the lower to a higher consciousness; the central pillar, of which Tiphareth is the centre, is the Pillar of Consciousness. Archetypal ideals are at this point brought into focus transmuted into ideas.

5. *The place of incarnation*, the birth place of the Divine Child and of spiritual consciousness. The inca'nation of the Spirit takes place by means of 'matter in a virgin state.'

6. *The place of sacrificial disincarnation:* the death of the body in the mystery of crucifixion. Tiphareth is the place of the Redeemer, the mediator who strives to bring the Kingdom into a state of equilibrium.

*

The images which help us discover the World of Mind, or Ethical World, have a distinctly mythological character. They coincide with widespread primordial ideas and abstract spiritual principles. They belong to all men; they are to be found in the myths and legends of all people and all times.

The collective image of God holds immense power and influence over our imagination. He is the link between the microcosm and the macrocosm, and through meditation on Him the soul of the individual man is opened to the One and the Eternal. It took a long period of cultural evolution to reduce the many gods to one God. Meditation on the One and Eternal is the key that opens the way to an increase of consciousness and a channel between the Creator and his creation.

It is, however, important to realize that whenever we open ourselves to any pure force and call upon the love of God, we receive it only through the channel of a mediator, a redeemer. Tiphareth is the sphere of the Redeemer and Raphael the Healer is its archangel.

The mandala, the magic circle of enlightenment and all-embracing unity, is the central symbol of individuality and of one centred in his higher Self. He stands in Tiphareth at the gateway of the archetypal world where he experiences directly the highest order and harmony, bringing revelation, realization and spiritual understanding in a flash of clarity, for Kether itself is reflected directly in Tiphareth. This is illumination, and many of us have experienced it briefly without recognizing it. It is no idealized state, but a very real experience which is possible for all of us if we find and open up our own deep centre to it.

The 'seeing' that we experience in Tiphareth is an illumination without form and its symbolism is expressed in terms of mystical experience. The vision we experience in Yesod consciousness, on the other hand, is a lower reflection of the Tiphareth vision, and it is expressed in symbolic representations or images, passed into the mirror of the subconscious mind, from which we translate them through dreams into terms of waking consciousness. It is valuable to understand these lower or astral visions in terms of metaphysics, otherwise we are in danger of endowing the symbols with undue authority as multiple gods, and becoming, in effect, spiritually hallucinated by them. When we do understand this, we can see how Tiphareth the mediator, the Son, redeems the pantheistic quality which prevents further growth beyond Yesod, by uniting that consciousness to an awareness of the transcendental father, Kether. True spiritual illumination consists in this – the introduction of the mind to a higher experience. One glimpse of this is enough to convince us of the reality of supra-physical existence.

When we touch the consciousness of Tiphareth it clarifies all the psychic or astral symbols. It is the voice which we hear with our inner ear, and through it we see with our inner eye the true visual representations of spiritual things. Through experiencing repeatedly this quickening and increased awareness, the individual develops a hyper-intuition and power of insight or spiritual perception. This higher consciousness is intuitive in its nature and contains no sensory imagery. Images of the astral plane are consumed through the fire of the Spirit, the dross of nature is cleared away and the initiate is left with the 'white heat' of pure consciousness. This white heat endures for only a short time, but during it the mind expands in such a way that subsequently it never wholly retracts. There follows a deep sense of joy and an enhanced capacity for life in general, as well as the power of realization and confidence in higher guidance.

*

Consciousness rises up from form to force on the Tree, and forces descend to form. Each must pass through Tiphareth, the centre of equilibrium. In this way the manifested forces to which Tiphareth opens the way – those of Chesed and Geburah – are reflected in Netzach and Hod respectively, so bringing the higher forces in us into the lower level of personality.

It is the swing and rhythm between Geburah and Chesed that creates a right balance in our social living. Both of these spheres have to do with the group soul, with mercy and justice and humanitarianism. The interaction between the apparent opposites of Geburah and Chesed produces equilibrium, not antagonism. Geburah's realism balances Chesed's idealism. Both are true servants of the Eternal.

Chesed and Geburah are symbolised for us by two kings, and represent the spiritual experiences of love and power respectively.

*

Chesed is the beneficent, loving father-king who continues the work of Chokmah the All-Begetter. Chesed organizes, preserves and builds up that which the All-Father has begotten. Chesed is seen as an enthroned king, a law-giver leading others not by violence, but by law and equity. Seated on his throne he expresses complete stability and ordered, merciful law. The virtue here is that of obedience and it is only through obedience that we can profit by his wise rule. Personal independence and egoism must be sacrificed to this greater good.

Chesed formulates the archetypal idea and makes the abstract principle concrete. He looks ahead and sees the things that must arise from given causes long before the first line is drawn on the plan or the first brick is laid. All creative work of the world is carried out through minds working in terms of Chesed. The mystical person functioning in Tiphareth will fall into error if he lacks the keys of Chesed. Chesed is the sphere of the apprehension by higher consciousness of an abstract concept which is subsequently brought down and made concrete in the light of experience in the lower self, the personality. The work of the great sages and masters is simply the making concrete of the abstract ideas conceived by the Logos, or the making of the unmanifest manifest. In the sphere of Chesed, the Loving Father in us receives the inspiration from the Logos which he works out on the planes of form.

The first meditation is the meditation of love in which you must so adjust your heart that you long for the weal and welfare of all beings, including the happiness of your enemies.

As in Tiphareth the relevant cross is the calvary cross of Christianity, so the cross associated with Chesed is the equal-armed cross, symbol of the four Elements in equilibrium.

*

Geburah is the might Warrior-King in his chariot, with the spiritual experience and vision of power. Geburah protects his people with the sword of righteousness, and ensures justice and commands respect. The person who can put the fear of God into us – to him we give our love and obedience. Geburah supplies that element of awe and fear of the Lord that is the beginning of wisdom. Geburah breaks down or dismantles what is outgrown, releasing energy into activity. Geburah is our courage and resolution in making the sacrifice for love which releases us from self-pity. He is the Celestial Surgeon with his clean-cutting scalpel who leaves the wound to heal cleanly, instead of the compromise that induces a septic condition. He is the pruning knife for anything that has outlived its usefulness. His courage and determination are needed wherever there is sloth and dishonesty. He reflects into Netzach, the Lady of Beauty, as the dragon-slayer and her lover.

Geburah is the dynamic element in life that overcomes obstacles. United with Binah the Great Mother, also called Understanding, Geburah perpetually breaks up the forms that Binah is perpetually binding – and without this she would bind the whole of creation into rigidity.

The right handling of this power of Geburah is a test of the highest spiritual integrity and self-discipline. We must develop an even temper and patience under all provocation; we must fight our adversary without malice, have mercy on the weak and defend the oppressed through Geburah. In doing so we receive our greatest experiences and a breaking down of our inflation and spiritual pride.

'He who struggles in the interest of self so that he himself
may be great or powerful, or rich, or famous
will have no reward.
But he who struggles for righteousness and truth
will have great reward,
for even his defeat will be a victory.'

A story: Aztec Judgement
(The experience of Tiphareth)

Man climbs the tree of life between Tonatiuh, Lord of the Sun and Life, and Mictlantecuhtli, Lord of the Underworld and Death. Around the root of the tree, which grows from symbols representing earth, air, fire and water, are assembled the constituent parts which came together at his conception – the fertilized seed, the hog of personality, the hawk of spirit, and the wings of his soul in a basket spangled with stars.

At the height of the tree, or death, shines the symbol of the sun itself, from which radiate four rays or paths. Thence spring the wings of the soul, released at last. While above, his various parts, split asunder by death, go to their destinies, to the left side of death the corpse tied in its shroud, and the beast which returns to the root of the tree; to the right side of life, the serpent, principle of consciousness, which came from the sun, and the spirit by which man is transfigured into the starry world.

Above all broods the Milky Way of countless suns.

A story: The Beggar and the King
(The experience of Chesed)

'I had gone a-begging from door to door in the village path, when thy golden chariot appeared in the distance like a gorgeous dream and I wondered who was this King of all kings!

'My hopes rose high and methought my evil days were at an end, and I stood waiting for the alms to be given unasked and for wealth scattered on all sides in the dust.

'The chariot stopped where I stood. Thy glance fell on me and thou camest down with a smile. I felt that the luck of my life had come at last. Then of a sudden thou didst hold out thy right hand and say, "What hast thou to give me?"

'Ah, what a kingly jest was it to open thy palm to a beggar to beg! I was confused and stood undecided, and then from my wallet I slowly took out the least little grain of corn and gave it to thee.

'But how great my surprise when at the day's end I emptied my bag on the floor to find a least little grain of gold among the poor heap. I bitterly wept and wished that I had had the heart to give thee my all.'

Rabindranath Tagore

5

THE WORLD OF SPIRIT

The following story is from the Chandogya Upanishad, *Thou Art That* – the experience of Essence or Being (Kether):

'Uddalaka spake unto Svetaketu, his son, saying, "Learn from me beloved. If one should smite upon the root of this great tree, beloved, it would sweat sap and live. If one should smite upon its top, it would sweat sap and live. Instinct with the Live Self, it stands full lush and glad.

"But if the Live One leaves one bough, it withers. If it leaves another bough, it withers. If it leaves a third bough, it withers. So know, beloved, the thing whence the Live One has departed does indeed die; but the Live One dies not. In this subtleness has this All its essence; it is the True; it is the Self; thou art it, Svetaketu."

"Let my lord teach me further," said the son.
"Be it so, beloved," the father replied.
"Bring from yonder a fig."
"Here it is, my lord."
"Break it."
"It is broken, my lord."
"What seest thou in it?"
"Here are but little seeds, my lord."
"Now break one of them."
"It is broken, my lord."
"What seest thou in it?"
"Naught, whatsoever, my lord."

'And he said to him: "*Of that subtleness which thou canst not behold*, beloved, is this great fig tree made. Have faith, beloved. *In this subtleness has this All its essence*; it is the True; it is the Self; thou art it, Svetaketu."

"Let my lord teach me further," said the son.

"Be it so, beloved," replied the father."Lay this salt in water, and on the morrow draw nigh to me." And he did so. Then he said to him: "Bring me the salt which thou laidst in the water yester eve."

He felt, but found it not; it was melted away.

"Drink from this end thereof. How is it?"

"It is salty."

"Drink from the midst. How is it?"

"It is salty."

"Drink from yonder end. How is it?"

"It is salty."

"Lay it aside and draw nigh to me." And he did so.

"It is still present," said he to him. "Herein forsooth thou canst not behold Being, beloved, but herein soothly it is. In this subtleness has this All its essence; it is the True; it is the Self; thou art it, Svetaketu." '

*

Throughout the centuries words, symbols, and images have been used to express or to attempt to express this Essence, this Truth that pervades us all. No two people ever quite cover the same conception of God. Our symbol of God is partly created through our background, through our daily life and daily needs, our language and the differences in circumstances and habits of our particular country. Very few of us ever reach perfect realization within our particular religion. We tend to see the Eternal Light through the mask imposed by our own thoughts and feelings. If we think of the plane of Spirit, or Essence, with which we are concerned in this talk, in terms of anything that we know or think that we know, we are liable to fall into grave error, for the World of Spirit lies beyond direct knowledge for us. Above Geburah and Chesed an abyss is said to lie across the Tree horizontally, and the spheres that are called supernal or supreme lie beyond it – the spheres of Kether, Chokmah and Binah which comprise the World of Spirit. (See top diagram on page 106.) This triad represents energies whose affinity lies entirely with the source of all in the limitless darkness against which we see the Tree, the Great Unmanifest or Unknown. Nevertheless the symbolism of the spheres is helpful and enables us to have a glimpse of that which transcends thought, time and place.

What is true of all symbols is particularly so in the case of this triad. They mask or veil that which they represent and are paradoxically simply of value in helping us to 'reduce the irreducible' to terms or ideas that are within our comprehension and which would otherwise be unthinkable. These three masks or veils of the transcendent realities, which belong to unknown territory, have a relationship through the pattern of the Tree of Life with the region of the known. Even such a veiled glimpse of the Unknown will help us to grow in wisdom. The fact that this veiled existence of 'Limitless Light' is outside the range of our *realization* does not prevent us being within the range of its influence. To turn our minds and hearts in the direction of the Light, even if we cannot reach it, is obviously of vital importance if we are to transcend the limitations of earth, Malkuth.

*

Images and symbols are powerful things. If we are to approach the Unknown we must work on them through intuition to reach Tiphareth, the point of initiation and seership.

All the spheres below the abyss are an expression of and a result of the union of the forces of Chokmah and Binah, the principle of generation.

In India the moment during the day when the hours of sun and darkness meet and which we call 'twilight' is referred to as the 'time of union.' In the yoga systems the sun current belongs to Chokmah and is known as Ida; the moon current belongs to Binah and is known as Pingala. The sun current is a fertiliser. It is the moon current belonging to the archetypal womb of Binah, the 'mother of all living,' that has the capacity to capture this life force and bring it into manifestation in Malkuth.

These active and passive principles are clearly reflected to us below the abyss in ways we can understand more easily.

When a man wants to use the moon forces of the feminine he attempts to get his sun force reflected. When a woman wants to use the sun forces she focuses them on herself and reflects them. Woman entices man through his desires and thus receives his sun-force and is impregnated. A man begets a child of a woman and thereby avails himself of her moon powers. Psychically this process of sexual polarity can only be carried out by shifting the level of consciousness onto a higher plane and working there.

On the earth plane our sexual polarity is fixed by our physical form, but on the subtle planes it is not fixed, but relative. This means that when we encounter that which is more forceful than ourselves, it is positive towards us and renders us negative or passive in relation to it. When we meet that which is less forceful, it is negative towards us, and we can assume the positive role in the relationship. By this we see that we must learn when to function as Chokmah and beget deeds, and when to function as Binah attracting others (and also our environment) to fertilize us. We can then produce and become productive of the new. This is the dynamic of all creativity.

It is very necessary to be constantly fertilized in this way and renewed by the medium in which we are working. Otherwise we tend to become completely sterile spiritually. There must be stimulus if we are to create new forms.

*

Binah is the builder of forms and the giver of death. Death is implicit in birth, as all forms born must eventually die. Binah is the vast, loving but also the terrible, bitter Mother. She is the Supernal Mother, the archetypal womb through which life comes into manifestation. Whatsoever, whomsoever provides a form to serve life is of Her. Form disciplines force with a merciless severity while the disembodied Spirit remains immortal and cannot grow old or die. Nevertheless She is an essential part of the natural life-cycle as is Mother Earth of the cycle of Nature. Any ascetic religion which denies both Mothers, seeing Mother as the enemy of Spirit, is going to bring about much human suffering as a result.

In some aspects Puritanism, Buddhism, Communism and Nazism all tend to contain this unhappy worship of the masculine at the expense of the feminine. The Truth is that both are equally holy, as together they form the basic rhythm of life. Binah is Understanding and the power to perceive the essence and interrelation of knowledge. She is the synthesis and relationship of all ideas, from the dense to the subtle. She is the awareness of the whole tree and not only the details of its parts. Faith rests in the letting go of intellectual knowledge and the seeing of the whole, the conscious result of superconscious experience. She is the 'sanctifying intelligence' of that which is holy and set apart. She brings forth the All but retains her virginity. Purity does not consist in emasculation; rather does impurity consist of a loss of control of vital forces.

*

Chokmah is Wisdom, the great stimulator of the universe, the Supernal Father and giver of life. 'The creative world,' 'dynamic force,' 'the voice of the logos' – all are descriptions of this sphere or centre of energy. 'Let there be light.' He is the illuminating influence of cosmic energy, the cosmic stimulus. Chokmah is pure energy, limitless and timeless. Binah gathers it and sets it to work.

A good many schoolgirls and schoolboys in the West first learned about sex from picking out passages in the Bible. Because we were not taught to treat reproduction as a sacred process and to approach it with reverence, these passages in the Bible were read with giggles and blushes. Indeed a Chinese girl interviewed recently said, 'But then you see, the joke in England is always sex. I mean that's the only thing that's funny in England. Not so with us in China.' Unfortunately sex was either a joke or it was equated with sin, through the blind prejudice of parents and teachers who were standing in the darkness of their own personal problems and difficulties. All too seldom were the amazing mysteries which are reflected in the act of generation revealed to us. One of the important secrets of the mysteries is the continuous interplay of sexual polarity at all levels.

Man is naturally physically and mentally active, but psychically and spiritually passive, and woman is physically and mentally passive but psychically and spiritually active – but their polarity of maleness and femaleness can in fact vary at different times between the participants on all of these planes bar the physical. When this law is not correctly understood there can be a disorder of sexual feeling breaking out into perverted and pathological expression. Within most of our relationships in life we sometimes play the positive or male and sometimes the negative or female role. Spiritually we are bi-sexual and our spiritual reactions are *not* fixed to masculine qualities or feminine qualities. Let us try to understand this a little more clearly by looking at the interplay of Chokmah and Binah as the essence of the partnership of Hod and Netzach, and as a pair of dynamic opposites that give us the fundamental key to sex or polarity in all its expressions and on all planes of existence.

*

Kether, as we have already seen from our Hindu story, is the Great Unknown, the Great Unknowable, whose centre is everywhere and whose circumference is nowhere. But the masking and unmasking of symbols and veils will reveal a great deal if we can extract a little of their meaningfulness:

> 'For who knows where or in what guise,
> The Lord Himself may come to Thee?
> In whatsoever name or form you desire to see God,
> in that very name and form you will see Him.
> Bow down and adore where others kneel,
> for where so many have worshipped
> the Lord will manifest Himself.'
>
> *Rama Krishna*

We cannot recognise the Truth through words unless they are illuminated by our personal experience. Unless we have *lived* the words that describe the experience at some time or other, there is no revelation.

Kether is the Concealed of the Concealed, the Primordial Point and innermost spiritual essence of Man and the Universe. Kether is the pure source of all energy and the reservoir of power, the all-pervading power. Though Kether is beyond our understanding, we are nevertheless open to its influence – and indeed each of us contains the divine spark of Kether.

In the spiritual triad the divine spark differentiates into Abba, 'Our Father,' and Ama, 'Our Mother.' So by this we see that sex is cosmic and spiritual with its roots in the three supernal spheres Kether, Chokmah and Binah. We also see that nature's laws are great, true and sanctified.

In spite of our surface fears the individual soul longs to be dissolved in the living ocean of the Great Mother, Ama, or to surrender and be consumed by the primal fire of Abba. As a child relates to its parents, so the individual soul finds its relationship to Chokmah or Binah: in the intimate tie of God 'Our Father' so well known to us, and in the even more intimate tie that finds God as Mother.

> 'My child, you need not know much in order to please me,
>   only love me dearly.
> Speak to me as you would to your Mother,
>   If she had taken you in her Arms.'

A mother's love justifies the existence of all her children, however unsympathetically they be judged by others. Each one of us has a place in the complete harmony of life and in the heart of the world-mother. To everyone, wherever they stand in life, using means that lie to hand, 'Fix thine heart upon the Lord thy God, and let thine Eyes look straight on.' If you recognize this, your core of strength and even your limitations will be wings upon your feet because then your actions become based on divine instinct.

> 'Dark Mother! Always gliding near with soft feet,
> Have none charted for Thee a chart of fullest welcome?'
>
> *Walt Whitman*

Chokmah and Binah, Siva and Shakti: the inspiration of their coming together in union is the great moment when we know, in a lightning flash, that the whole of what we call life, time, nature, in fact all that is without as well as the experience of all that we call 'within' is God. In other words, the soul opening its eyes at last upon the world sees God everywhere.

6

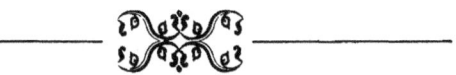

DYNAMISM AND MAGNETISM: THE FUNCTIONING OF THE TREE

The Tree of Life is not fixed or static. It is organic – a living, functioning entity. Its whole functioning is empowered by the interaction of the principles of dynamism and magnetism. These principles or energies are rooted in the primal spheres of Chokmah and Binah, which head the side pillars of the Tree. It is by way of these pillars that the forces of the two primal spheres give rise to further interaction of opposites in the lower pairs of Chesed and Geburah, and Netzach and Hod. (See lower diagram on page 106.)

This positive-and-negative relationship of two forces – one active and one passive – is also the pattern of the relationship between the two upper worlds and the two lower worlds – between the higher Self and the lower self.

Only a symbolic conception such as The Tree of Life can place the centre of gravity in that other infinite world which is spiritual and dynamic. Through it we can learn to see everywhere around us the signs and symbols of this other world, divine and infinitely mysterious, which lies beyond that which is finite and transitory.

Symbolism is the vision of the infinite in the finite. The power of the symbol renders the finite transparent and allows us to see the infinite through it. When the whole outward order is symbolically sanctified, the horizons of the finite world are no longer restricted.

Reality is necessarily at a deeper level of existence. The dynamic penetration of the spiritual world into the natural world and the divine manifestation of the bond that unites them is the constant victory of Grace. Forces can arise in us from the depths of the spirit, capable of transforming us and freeing us from all the external attachments that hold us in bondage.

I cannot possibly be indifferent as to whether events and happenings in my life – and on which my fate depends in time and also in eternity – have their prototype in the spiritual world. It is of vital importance to me whether God is a dynamic and living reality in my life or merely an abstract idea. The mystical meeting of soul with Christ which transformed Saul into Paul the Apostle is an encounter which all of us have the possibility of experiencing for ourselves. Only such a spiritual experience can truly liberate us. Revelation is revolution, not evolution. It is a dynamic awakening and a new orientation of consciousness. Personal consciousness is not a limitation of spirit by the body, neither is the borderline between consciousness and unconsciousness static. Consciousness itself is active and dynamic. All spiritual experience reveals to us the existence of cosmic consciousness which is unlimited.

Worldly wisdom is associated with the direction of our consciousness towards visible things. This is gradually dissolved through increasing spiritual awareness of invisible things and in a worldly sense we become fools. 'For the wisdom of this world is foolishness with God.' So we must become fools in order to become spiritually wise. Becoming a fool means to be receptive, passive, silent and spellbound while the grace of God is alone active within.

The source of the Tree and of life is a perfect one*ness* of which we are absolutely unconscious. The idea of duality or opposites is secondary to it and only appeared with the first glimmer of manifestation. In this sense life is a whole; nothing can be added to it and nothing can be subtracted from it, the whole being the part and the part the whole. This harmonious whole is the totality of divine potency. The error that we call 'sin' – any working against the divine laws – necessarily destroys such a unity for us and the fruit becomes separated from the Tree. Creative transformation is therefore a total process in which the creative principle manifests as power or dynamism in relation to the centre of the whole personality. This centre must be venerated by us as the hidden treasure that in our humble outward form conceals a fragment or Divine Spark of the Godhead and Crown of Kether.

Love is the prime moving power of the creating Spirit, but its manifestation as form is necessary for it to be expressed. This dynamic spirit of life which seeks expression in our individual lives has no other intention than 'that we might have life, and that we might have it more abundantly.' The good impulse or deed guides the flow of blessing, which springs from the superabundance of life in the higher spheres, into the secret channels leading into the lower and outer worlds. Through our acts of devotion we are able to link the invisible and mysterious to the visible and practical. To the extent that we lack a conscious unity with this one eternal life this is, as yet, only imperfectly apparent. The development of consciousness and the increase of spiritual awareness in us is contingent on a primordial light and a pre-established order.

Our study of the Tree of Life will, if we are receptive to the truths it contains, awaken our intuitive imagination, enabling us to become increasingly sensitive to ideas emanating from the supreme source. We are then gradually brought into greater harmony and unison with it. Intuition should use symbols as thinking uses words – first the symbol then the elucidation, each symbol elucidating the other by means of its relative position on the Tree. Formulation of the image and the vibration of the spoken name (for a word is a type of symbol) put the student in touch with the forces behind each sphere of the Tree. Coming into touch in this way, one's consciousness is illumined and one's being is energised by the force contacted. Contemplation of the symbols brings about illumination. As long as each stage is in the right relation to all the others it is sacred and good. Otherwise, if we fail to remain in the original context of all things created, in which each of us has our place, we become isolated and cut off from our spiritual roots. It is then that we endeavour to take God's place, with the result that we create an unreal world for ourselves which is full of false contexts.

If we can only retain this awareness of the whole Tree of Life we can then see clearly that everything is life's expression and life's experience. Then there can never be the fear of losing anything. On the contrary, this clarity shows us the value of giving most and taking least. Since this life essence manifests itself in various *forms*, our experiences of this life naturally vary according to the nature and potentialities of the form. These experiences also tend to be partial because of the natural limitations of form. No 'form of expression' can therefore ever be regarded as the whole of life or truth. Again it is not difficult to see why it is that the person who is capable of being alone with God is the true centre of the community. She or he has reached the stage at which true communion is possible.

We have seen how Kether is negative in relation to the unmanifest but positive in relation to the whole Tree. In the same way the present is negative to the past, and positive to the future. We learn from studying the I Ching that the underlying idea of the Whole is the idea of change or becoming. In the *Analects,* Confucius, standing by the river, said, 'Everything flows on and on like this river, without pause, day and night.

She or he who perceives the meaning of change then focuses attention on the eternal law at work in all change and not on transitory individual things. Tao is the principal of the 'One in the many'. The idea of a primal beginning was represented in the I Ching by the symbol of a circle, this circle or wholeness being divided into the Dark and the Light, Yin and Yang. This Yin and Yang, or the female and male primal principles, represent the duality present in the world. The world of being rises out of their change and interplay; the art of living is the ability to function both ways on alternating currents. Change is the continuous transformation of the one force into the other. This change, being subject to the universal law, is therefore meaningful and not meaningless.

Lao-tse taught that every event in the visible world is the effect of an 'image' or 'idea' or 'archetypal idea' in the unseen world. Everything that manifests itself on earth is an expression of an event in a world beyond our sense perception. Thus humanity is linked with heaven and with earth, or with the world of ideas and the world of visible things. To the extent that there is a real expansion of consciousness in us, to that extent we have access to these ideas or truths through direct intuition. Discerning the seed of things to come, we can learn to foresee the future and to understand the past. All outward forms and expressions of natural, physical life are symbols of the spirit. They are the reflections, the images and the signs of a very profound and inner reality, our spiritual world. They all express the dynamic nature of this Divine Spirit, they are all mysterious and infinite. What is dynamic cannot tolerate or remain subordinate to the static.

The title of this talk is 'Dynamism and Magnetism.' We know that the word 'dynamic' means a causal and a moving force or imminent energy, and the word 'magnetic' means to attract as if by a magnet. We also know that the earth itself possesses magnetic properties. The I Ching expresses the creative action of the deity in terms of the Earth Mother, seeing them as complementary to one another. In the creative man, the feminine principle of 'anima' becomes the motive for transformation; indeed in every creative individual the accent is unquestionably on the receptive or feminine component If we look into this we will see that the preservation of receptivity at all costs is indeed the preservation of our own individuality against convention and all worldly authority. To be receptive is to be open to experiences of all kinds and to keep alive the creative spirit or life force that flows eternally into the world.

Every transformative or creative process involves a stage of possession and magnetism. When we are attracted, moved, captivated and finally spellbound by anything or anyone, we surrender and allow ourselves to be possessed. Without the fascination and emotional tension connected with this stage of being, no creative process, where real attention and concentration are necessary, is possible. Of course all such situations are highly dangerous, but unless we have the courage to accept the risk involved, no real achievement is possible. It is in this sense that Jung uses the term 'participation mystique'. It is when something or someone becomes alive for us or magnetizes us that this something becomes symbolic and speaks to us in a new way. In other words, this indeed is the language of love in the sense that it reveals to us the unknown.

All great contents of the world and the collective unconscious contain archetypal experiences and the vital seed of transformation. The timeless moment, the moment of bliss, of recognition, is where the psychic inward image and the outward physical image appear as one original symbolic unity. There is no longer a split between what is inside us and what is outside us. Here is a moment of total awareness without division, a moment of perfect harmony and happiness. The growth of consciousness, spiritual perception and the consequent upsurge of love can only develop during these moments of bridging and linking with the creative powers of the unconscious.

Love as we recognise it fully is the dynamism of the creating spirit. The inherent nature of the spirit consists of the eternal interaction of love and beauty as the active and passive polarity of Being. The power of all divine mental images starts into action the universal law of attraction. This law of attraction or magnetism gives rise to the principle of growth. It is an invariable truth that our individual life will take its whole tone and colour from our spiritual conception of God It is necessarily through the personal element that the beginning of the specific action of the divine spirit or universal law relative to that particular individual takes place.

The danger of the individual within the crowd is that one easily becomes the victim to one's suggestibility. Within a crowd or a group we tend to identify, to shelve responsibility and at the same time to be without fear. Whatever is proposed by the whole crowd tends to draw us into agreement with it. Mass intoxication does affect and produce changes in the individual but without going very deep, and the change seldom lasts. Here is another form of magnetism or 'participation mystique' where in identifying with the mass you become caught up in a web of mutual unconscious relationship and are borne along with it. Ritual on the other hand is quite a different matter. Within the ritual it is possible to have a very real individual experience. It is only where the unconscious is not expressed through spiritual symbolism that the collective psyche has this hypnotic effect and draws us under its spell. What happened in Germany in the Second World War is a supreme example of this.

The other magnetic experience that we witness everyday is the type of 'participation mystique' that exists between my personality and the objects around me. To the extent that my possessions are carriers of my projections, they become much more than what they are in themselves. Here we have the problem of 'mine-ness' – my house, my books, my child, my car, etc. etc. I am affronted for this reason if 'my things' are not treated with sufficient respect due to my identification

– 'whoever damages my car, damages me.' If I give something away that is precious and belongs to me, it is a form of self-sacrifice. All absolute giving is total loss from the start and a form of sacrificial love. Spiritually speaking, when the offering is the offerer himself – his or her essence or inner nature – there we have a true mystical unity of all parts of the sacrificial act. And it is the divine source itself which has magnetized us into surrender, because the power that draws us direct has become for us so much greater than the power exercised through any transitory form. So is the weaving and rending of the veil repeated for all eternity.

*

The Tree in Function: the two interacting powers

Magnetism	*Dynamism*
Negative	Positive
Passive	Active
Static force	Kinetic force
Receptive	Stimulating
Latent power	Dynamic power
Organising, stabilising force	Unorganised, uncompensated force
All-potential	All-potent
Down-breaking	Up-building
Supernal Mother	Supernal Father
Pillar of Severity	Pillar of Mercy

*

The functioning of the spheres

The same dynamic functions in the relating of the various spheres of the Tree. Each sphere is negative or feminine in relation to its predecessor – whence it emanates and receives the divine influence – in the down-flow of creative energy. And each sphere is positive or masculine to its successor, to whom it transmits the divine influence. Therefore each sphere is bi-sexual, a magnet, one pole of which is positive and the other negative.

A sphere in the feminine Pillar of Severity is well-dignified when it is functioning in its negative-feminine aspect and ill-dignified when it is functioning positively in a masculine sense, e.g. the receptive feminine equals stability and endurance, but when positive it becomes actively aggressive (in woman as negative animus).

A sphere in the masculine Pillar of Mercy is well-dignified when it is functioning in its positive aspect and ill-dignified when it is functioning in its negative aspect, e.g. the creative masculine orders and preserves harmony, but when negative it becomes sentimental (in man as negative anima).

An Indian Parable of Two Friends: Dioscuri
(the dual motive of mortal and immortal)

Behold, upon the selfsame tree,
Two birds, fast-bound companions, sit.
This one enjoys the ripened fruit,
The other looks, but does not eat.

On such a tree my spirit crouched,
Deluded by its powerlessness,

Consciousness dissolves in vision.

from: Hui Ming Ch'ing

*

Till seeing with joy how great its Lord,
It found from sorrow swift release.

from: Shevetashvatana Upanishad

*

A luminosity surrounds the world of spirit.
We forget one another when, still and pure,
   we draw strength from the Void.
The Voice is filled with the light of the Heart
   of Heaven.

7

VIRTUE AND VICE

'Life and Death,' said Confucius, 'existence and non-existence, success and non-success, poverty and wealth, virtue and vice, good and evil report, hunger and thirst, warmth and cold – all these revolve upon the changing wheel of Destiny. Day and night they follow one upon the other, and no man can say where each one begins. Therefore they cannot be allowed to disturb the harmony of the organism, nor enter into the soul's domain. Swim however with the tide, so as not to offend others. Do this day by day without break, and live in peace with mankind. Thus you will be ready for all contingencies, and may be said to have your talents perfect.'

'And virtue without outward form; what is that?' said his disciple.

'In a water-level,' said Confucius, 'the water is in a most perfect state of repose. Let that be your model. The water remains quietly within, and does not overflow. It is from the cultivation of such harmony that virtue results. And if virtue takes no outward form, man will not be able to keep aloof from it.'

Without harmony and balance within, there is a one-sided attitude of consciousness resulting in compensating dreams of a disturbing character. Where there is this one-sided attitude, there is also the fear of its opposite. Desire for, and a one-sided drive towards personal success produces its opposite of fear of failure and other fears. For fear has to do with punishment and he who fears is not perfect in love.

'If anyone says "I love God" and hates his brother, he is a liar; for he who does not love his brother whom he has seen, cannot love God whom he has not seen.'

Whenever a feeling is voiced with truth and frankness, there you find spiritual attraction affecting those who are inwardly receptive. Something then emanates from the heart, and exerts an influence.

Since earliest times all positive goodness emanating from the Heart in whatever form or expression has been known as 'virtuous' and of the 'angels.' All negative evil emanating from destructive egotistical thinking and compulsive aggressive instincts has been known as 'vicious' and of the 'demons' or devils.

In Dante's *Divine Comedy* he gives all sorts of names to various devils, e.g. Barbaricciais called Malicious and Cayhazzo, The Snarler or one who snarls at other people. In early times every person was considered to contain two distinct demons, a good one and a bad one, but later it was recognised that good and bad alike proceeded at different times from the demon of each individual. This differentiation between the beneficent and malignant qualities emanating from the individual resulted in their representation as the Good Spirit or Guardian Angel and the Evil Spirit or Devil of Christian theology.

The essential distinction between the divine and the human that now seem to us so fundamental was not and *is not* so with primitive peoples. Notions of visible and invisible worlds are both in their case animistic. Similarly there are primitive stratas in our own unconscious that will produce fears and nightmares of an instinctive animistic and superstitious nature. To the extent that we have not developed any spiritual awareness and consciousness of our divine and higher nature, to that extent there is the danger in crises of, for example, hysterical fears, frenzies, and ravings. Slavonic mythology in particular is rich in malignant male and female demons, gloomy shadows of old nature myths and degraded forms of what were once great deities of pagan religions. Particular animals have been favourite hosts for demons to inhabit, e.g. the serpent, the cat, the hedgehog, the hare, the fox, the he-goat, the raven, the wolf.

It is for this reason that such animals are very potent when they appear, sometimes in dreams of a frightening nature. The medieval belief that various gods of the old heathen world were the degraded angels or devils of Scripture, led to them being represented in the fantastic gargoyles of many of the churches at that time.

Jewish monotheism rejected the notion of two ultimate principles of good and evil but stressed the unseen divine reality and dynamic unity underlying the multiplicity of evil. The name 'Satan', meaning adversary and also the name 'Lucifer' came to express all forms that opposed and fought against the Divine Essence, love and goodness. The New Testament writes freely of the activity of the devil (in this respect) in all human affairs.

Today Hell itself is no longer a place but a state of mind and a tragic view is presented of Satan. Milton in *Paradise Lost* shows us this tragedy of Satan most clearly. Here Satan is an archangel, still magnificent in his downfall but with all his great gifts turned to hatred and darkness. The gifts are still there but mis-directed. He is no monster, but a vast, flaming spirit capable of weeping and tears for his followers, sustaining them by his own self-generated force of hate and planning revenge on God through the destruction of mankind.

We have all experienced this great tragedy of wasted and mis-directed gifts in our own lives, of our passions turned destructive instead of constructive, of the 'wastelands' of T.S. Eliot. The fear generated in one another *of* one another creates the growing of thick skins and rhinoceros hides, with protection through conformity and stupidity and smug self-centred complacency. We catch this disease when we are puffed up with pride and malice because the devil is a 'distorted' and therefore a 'distorting' mirror. Satan, of course, fails ultimately in his destructiveness simply because he is incapable of grasping the true nature of Good. It can never be grasped by the head but only received through the vulnerability and thin sensitive skin of the open heart. The Devil of modern times taints and cheapens everything good and noble. He convincingly colours and distorts. Like the primitive peoples we still prefer to hunt him down through a material vehicle separated from ourselves or, in other words, to find a scapegoat. Hence the talk of war and atom bombs. This is our desperate effort to clear the air so that we can breathe more freely. We try to transfer the evil from ourselves to another.

Christ the Scapegoat was nailed to the Cross. He became the spiritual food and nourishment that can increase our spiritual strength and mental health. He is the fire of passion to be used constructively. He is our invisible guardian and protector, our link with the higher spheres. He is essentially the centre of the Tree in that He is this underlying Unity that links us all beneath the multiplicity of Evil manifesting outwardly and the duplicity of the enemy within. He is the microcosmic Tree of Life linking us to the invisible prototype and macrocosmic Tree of Life.

We have all found that with the desire not to be something there comes a conflict of the opposites. It is a fact we have all experienced – that the desire of the will not to be this, but to be that, produces immediate conflict within. Indeed most of us accept the fact of this conflict as the natural process of life and often see this eternal struggle between what is and what we think we should be as something even noble and idealistic. Freedom comes not through the conflict of its opposite but through the understanding of what is. But we cannot reach the understanding so long as our mind is concerned with changing what is into its opposite. Indeed the wilful desire to alter something into its opposite can never bring about fundamental change. The desire or will to be the opposite of something is exactly the same as being it, and to perceive the truth of what is without seeking to change it from this to that is to avoid the merely superficial. To understand the full significance of this fact is to bring about a radical transformation. As long as we are busy comparing, judging, in order to seek a result, there is no possibility of change, but merely a perpetuation of the conflict. To struggle against something, against a habit for example, is merely to give it more force. To be fully aware of the habit without choosing and cultivating an opposite habit, is to end the habit.

The true secret of natural goodness lies in the true balance and recognition of all contending opposites. It is in the balance of extremes - and not 'the pull of opposites' which tears the psyche apart between this thing and that thing, between good and evil, between past and future.

*

Each sphere of the Tree brings as a gift to evolution a particular quality inherent in its energy – a virtue. This is an ideal aspect of the sphere's energy, but if carried to excess, that very quality overbalances and takes the form of a vice directly corresponding to the nature of the quality. In Kether and Chokmah, however, the spheres before the energy emerges in Binah, there is no corresponding vice; they are represented by virtues only.

It is one of the lessons that the Tree offers us, to recognise the proper use of each virtue and to learn to develop and manage it in ourselves in due measure so as to keep from being drawn to its opposite, the corresponding vice.

In the last paper we have seen the rhythm between dynamism and magnetism in relation to the Tree working down from the higher to the lower spheres. In this paper, bearing in mind all that has been said, we should look at the virtue and vice connected with each sphere, starting with Malkuth and working upwards, the direction of attainment.

Malkuth: Here we see that the virtue is 'discrimination' and the vice inertia. We learn that whatever in life is no longer of any use must be excreted, only retaining that which is helpful and spiritually nourishing. Psychological constipation and sluggishness is the hanging on to that which is redundant. It is the retaining on the material plane of that which is valueless to us spiritually and which therefore costs us a great deal in this respect. It was Freud who pointed out that miserly people sometimes suffer from constipation, and often in his interpretation of their dreams he associated money with faeces. So we must learn to 'let go,' to stop clinging to the past, to other people and to objects. We must learn to breathe fresh new air, to awaken from our sluggishness and inertia, and to sacrifice the trivial and unimportant to the spiritually important. To do this we must use our discrimination and develop it, as every true sacrifice of this kind lays up treasure in heaven so to speak. How often do we allow 'heaven-sent opportunities' to slip by? We miss the bus and waste them. It is we who are constantly failing to act on our God-given impulses and ideas. We evade and avoid and allow ourselves to be corrupted by the superficial and unimportant.

Yesod: Here we have the virtue of 'independence' and the vice of 'idleness.' It is the unconscious that works behind the field of consciousness. It is negative thinking and idle thoughts that create all sorts of inhibitions and obstruct our freedom of movement. Because of inhibitions created by ideology (Hod) or emotions (Netzach), we fail to see or detect the movement of the enemy within, with the immediacy of the moon casting its reflection on the water. This immediate spiritual perception and 'seeing' is the all important factor. With this right kind of independence we receive strength in our earth contacts, also material happiness and gain if we are adequate to deal with it. We may also receive emotional well-being. To fall into idleness and to be unaware is to fall into despair and subsequently cruelty.

Hod: Here we have 'truthfulness' as our virtue and 'dishonesty' as the vice. There is a Zen verse that goes like this:-

> 'It is mind that deludes Mind,
> For there is no other mind.
> O Mind, do not let yourself
> Be misled by mind.'

The true Mind is to be protected from the false one in order to preserve its purity and freedom unspoiled. The knowledge through Hod must be linked to a refreshing and vitalizing force from Netzach, stimulated through intercourse with friends, with whom one should apply the truths of life. An idea, however worthy and desirable in itself, becomes a disease when the mind is obsessed with it. Mercury or Hermes is the god of science and books, but in his negative aspect he is the god of thieves and cunning rogues. The danger in Hod is the stealing of ideas and of remaining 'all theory and no practice.'

Netzach: Our virtue with Netzach is 'unselfishness' and our vice is 'lust.' It is through Netzach that the elemental forces obtain access to consciousness. Here is the possibility of harmony with nature forces and psychic forces through our instincts and emotions. Aphrodite the goddess of love gives us creative expression through the arts and appreciation of beauty, but only if we are free of all selfish ulterior considerations are we capable of dissolving the hardness of egotism through steadfastness. Those who lack inner stability and need amusement and distraction, will always find the opportunity for indulgence. Egotism and cupidity isolate men. Only through an attitude of devotion can we be stirred by intuition of the One Creator of all living beings. The vice of lust or merely stimulated desire expresses itself today through the medium of inferior films and television and insensitive novels and newspapers. To meet the needs of the human soul for etheric and mental interchange we need the right intellectual and spiritual polarization.

Tiphareth: The virtue here is 'devotion to the work of the higher' (regeneration); the vice is 'pride,' with its roots in egotism. So long as we are self-centred we cannot be centred in the Self and made ONE. It is a very different matter to try to possess a thing to being One with it. To attempt to possess the higher is appropriation; it is spiritual pride, which leads to obsession and fanaticism. The devotion needed here is limitless sympathy, perfect love, and perfect reciprocity.

'Let he who would be the greatest among you
be the servant of all.'

Here devotion leads to higher consciousness and to the love for something higher than self. It is the devotion which rises to adoration and total sacrifice of egotism.

Geburah: 'Courage' is our virtue, and 'destruction' our vice. In Zen we learn that when there is no obstruction of whatever kind, the swordsman's movements are like flashes of lightning; or again they are likened to a clear mirror reflecting images. If in his mind there is any shadow of doubt, any sense of fear or insecurity, this indecision at once reveals itself in the sword's movements and this indeed means a defeat. The sword is the symbol of the invisible spirit keeping the mind and body in full activity. It is the spirit of the Tree itself without which there would be no splitting buds, no blossoming flowers, and therefore no fruit. The swordsman must not harbour anything external and superfluous in his mind; his mind must be perfectly purged of all egocentric emotions. When this is carried out the mind itself is 'lost' and no devil can trace its whereabouts or enter. He has become the teaching itself and there is now no separation between the learner and the learning. If the learner becomes the slave of his learning then his knowledge destroys himself and others. Here taking his spiritual courage in both hands he must become the defender of the weak and oppressed. Only if he acts in this way from his own and not the higher intention will there be danger of the ego carrying him into sheer destructiveness and cruelty.

Chesed: The virtue is 'obedience,' and the vice 'hypocrisy and tyranny.' This sphere contains the Holy Powers from which emanate the spiritual virtues and exalted essences. Chesed is the receptive intelligence which is obedient to Kether. Over-insistence on this obedience leads to the unbalanced forces of bigotry, hypocrisy and tyranny.

Binah: The virtue of Binah is 'silence.' The vice here is 'avarice,' and it is a clinging to life and form, an inability to become submerged totally. No form can be infinite or eternal. The silence is a state of containment, sustained total receptivity.

Chokmah: The virtue of Chokmah is pure and utter devotion.

Kether: The virtue of Kether is attainment.

8

THE TURNING POINT

As we become more aware of the higher levels of the Tree, and so make contact with the principles there, we gradually bring the Tree that is ourselves into better balance. Illumination and revelation bring moments when we exclaim joyfully, 'I see!,' by which we mean 'I understand.' In those moments we experience a sense of liberation and of relaxation – because we have in fact freed our consciousness from the heavy hold of the lower worlds. We have raised the centre of gravity of the Tree to its true place – Tiphareth – so that for a short time the whole pattern functions in free natural balance, poised and weightless – as we ourselves become and feel at that time. After each of these experiences we are irreversibly changed in some degree. We have grown a little, and opened the way for further growth.

Somewhere in the course of repeating these experiences of en-light-enment and comprehension we reach a point where the emphasis of our concerns and being has shifted once and for all from the lower to the higher. When this happens our true individuality, our essence, predominates in our being – as it was originally intended.

'The approach is not by a physical progression, but by flashes of succeeding light, and these are not corporal but spiritual . . . the soul must seek the light by following the light.'

*

A turning point is a moment of change, a change of movement or of direction, a change of substance. It is an overflow, a sparking off. You become more balanced; you suddenly feel a greater sense of equilibrium, of troubles dissolving into thin air, mountains becoming molehills, anxieties and fears vanishing suddenly like a puff of smoke. Your heart suddenly begins to overflow with love and compassion or with joy. You are suddenly inspired, something strikes you, illuminates you, fires you with enthusiasm. All these can be turning points leading to *The* Turning Point. These 'little turning points' are stepping stones leading from identification with our exterior being to our interior Be-ing, from the circumference to the Centre as it were. It is the process of accretion or assimilation, mystically known as 'eating.'

There is a great deal of difference between dis-continuous change and continuous change, between casually struck notes and real harmony, between what is chaotic and what is cosmic. Continuous change is a series of turning points via which we reach spiritual wholeness or holiness. The relation in which we stand to our source is a deeply mysterious one. Somewhere we know that there is a higher principle of activity within us and that we feel impelled to reconcile it with the Power that brought us into the world. It is essentially a question of attunement rather than attainment. Then the freedom we enjoy becomes creative instead of destructive in character.

Each time you go through a strong mental and psychological reaction to someone or something, it is because you are confronted with some aspect of yourself in another form. You will have no peace until you have 'eaten it' or assimilated it into your own being and thereby made conscious what was previously unconscious. The psychological rule says that when an inner situation is not made conscious, it happens outside as fate, i.e. when the individual does not become conscious of his inner contradictions, the world must perforce act out the conflict and be torn into opposite halves.

Both the primitive man at one end of the scale and the highly developed spiritual man at the other are aware in their different ways that the self is only artificially isolated from the rest of the universe. There is a deep and fundamental impulse within each one of us to identify ourselves with all forms of life. On the surface our thoughts and feelings become conditioned to a far greater degree than most of us suspect, until we begin to suffer unbearable tension. It is only after much adaptation and discomfort that we begin to glimpse the real state of affairs. This is the beginning of our series of turning points and true inner unfoldment. Each assimilation of previously unpalatable truths about ourselves increases our vision, our capacity to 'see.'

'We needs must love the Highest when we see it.'

The Higher Self begins to 'eat up' the little self, however difficult it is sometimes to swallow. The mind is like the moon, deriving its light of consciousness from the Self. The Self resembles the sun. Hence when the Higher Self begins to shine, the mind, like the moon, becomes useless.

Hearing helps the intellectual understanding of the Truth. Meditation makes the understanding clear. Contemplation brings about realization of the Truth. The intellect sinks into the ego and the ego into the Self.

The variety of phenomena perceived is of 'the 'outgoing' mind. The 'in going' or 'Heart-going' mind is called 'the resting mind.'

All of us are seeing God always but we do not know it. We see, but yet see not, that God is perpetual consciousness – 'That which sees.'

The finite and infinite pass into each other and become one when we let go of all ideas of relativity. In our relative way of thinking generally the two are sharply differentiated and there is no way of unifying them. It is our habit to split one solid Reality into two. The point between, or as Eckhart calls it, 'the little point left by God, is that point at which when it is struck we experience 'satori,' the state of ineffable unity and harmony. To experience 'satori' means to find ourselves standing at the point where we can look in two directions, towards God and toward the creation. The 'little point' is a kind of axis around which we and God move. This truth will be experienced when we actually reach the point, in other words, the point where the finite is infinite and the infinite is finite. The eye, the inner eye by which I see God in all things, is the same eye through which God sees me – one in seeing, one in knowing, one in loving. If I see blue or white the seeing of my eyes is identical with what is seen. The seeing is the seen and the seen *is* the seeing: I sink at that point into the eternity of the Divine Essence.

The turning point can turn us in the direction of the Godhead and also turn us in the direction of our own creatureliness. Now we know God as the true God directly and not through knowledge about Him. Here all ideas, all distinctions, all comparisons are let go, leaving God to be in Himself and with Himself.

Meister Eckhart defines such a person who has 'turned': 'So I say that the Aristocrat (Edel) is one who derives his being, his life and his happiness from God alone, with God and in God and not all from knowledge, perfection, or love of God, or any such thing. Thus our Lord says very well, that Life Eternal is to know God as the only true God and not that it is through knowledge that God may be known.'

A creative association is also gradually established between ourselves and others. This creative impulse is a reflex of the presence within us of a superior power that challenges our accustomed self and gives us no rest from now on. The turning point of the soul towards God is made by the whole person, the heart and mind together.

When we were upset with another person's hostility or anger we used to say, 'change and then I will love you.' Now we know that only the change or turning point in ourselves can bring about the moment when we realize, 'love someone, and he or she will change.' Crossing over the chasm we become the other person's possession. When love persists even when there is no return, then *that* feeling is pure and of the nature of cosmic love. Love of humanity in the abstract and dislike of the particular human being is defective love. It is love at a distance and not the love of immediate service. Love cannot be utilitarian, only loving those who are useful or pleasing in personality. It must be all-embracing, otherwise we are merely loving the experience and not the person.

The important thing is trusting in God and waiting for His grace without impatience. Reliance on God is alone true Self-reliance. Goodness is not a possession. It is the possessor. Truth and goodness are essentially the same.

Sri Ramana Maharshi once expressed the Christian crucifixion in Eastern terms:

> 'The body is the Cross; the ego is Jesus the "Son of Man"; when he is crucified, He is resurrected as the Son of God, which is the glorious real Self. In other words, one must lose the ego in order to love.'

The point of surrender of the ego is the total recognition of a higher, over-ruling power. The heart centre is therefore not only a scene of struggle, but also the beginning of true altruism. Here the chord of Self is struck in order to make music for others. Life must now not only live for itself, but also live for others. The trunk and branches of the tree are for individuated self, but the blossoms and fruit are for others. As with all trees, reproduction is hastened by wounding, and sacrifice and surrender is the condition of a new and richer life. Each time a fruit of the tree falls to the ground, the outer casing decays but the seeds at the centre are a promise of immortality. They are also a reminder that man's true growth is through the eternal communion with the spiritual forces constantly and eternally issuing from the heart of God. Your thoughts may change but you don't change. Keep hold of the unchanging you.

> 'That which dwells in the hearts of one and all
> as Pure Awareness is the overself, so when
> the heart melts in love and the Cave of the Heart
> where He shines is reached,
> then the Eye of Awareness opens and He is
> realized as the real Self.'

The Highest Praise of God and the most pleasing to Him, is not that He is the Supreme Lord of all creation, but that He is the most beloved of all, as the Self in the Heart. Then He Himself becomes the consumer of the Ego. Devotion is effortless, without strain. There is no command to love Him. We do so because we cannot help it.

A Zen story: The Hermit

Tokuzan was walking through the market of a near-by town. He noticed in particular a vendor of millet-seed vociferously shouting the virtues of his commodity. Finally he entered into conversation with the man, and was surprised by his wise remarks.

'For a vendor of millet-seed you make an admirable philosopher,' he observed.

'As a hermit I have plenty of time for meditation,' the man agreed.

'Did you say "hermit"?' asked the Master, thinking he had misheard.

The man waved his hand to indicate the jostling crowd and recited: 'Owing to the exigencies of circumstance, my last remnants of privacy have been removed. Now, my seclusion is complete.'

'Remarkable,' said Tokuzan. 'Will you please explain?'

The man continued. 'Long time since, I wished to retire from the world and become a hermit. However, I was smitten with the love-sickness and took a wife instead. She bore me many children, including several fine but noisy sons. Still I longed for seclusion in which to meditate, but the demands my family necessarily made upon me increased, and my leisure hours became less and less. Finally, when all my time was occupie, I went away, and now I live alone in the bosom of my family and the clamour of the market. I doubt if I shall come back.'

He proffered a handful of millet-seeds.

Tokuzan marvelled as he accepted the seeds. 'In the whole of China I should say you have no equal.'

Good-humouredly, the man remonstrated. 'In the whole of China there is no one else but I.'

9

LEFT HAND, RIGHT HAND

We have probably all heard of the expression, 'the left hand does not know what the right hand is doing,' which of course originated from the passage in St Matthew:

> 'But when thou doest alms, let not thy left hand know what thy right hand doeth, that thy alms may be in secret.'

Nevertheless on all other occasions it is very important to know what both are doing, so that there can be a real growth of consciousness in order that we become totally aware and not split or divided. Today most of us think of life in terms of problems. This means that our psychic life is composed of a complex pattern of reflections, experience and doubts that are quite alien to the unconscious, instinctive, and primitive side of our nature.

Many of us fight against greater clarity and try hard to deny these difficulties by turning away from them. We cling to old forms, childish illusions and egoistic habits instead of allowing the fluidity of the spirit within us to break them up and lead us out into freer life. So many things that should have been lived out fully at the time lie in the lumber-room of our dusty memories and personal and social attitudes. In middle life our principles tend to harden and begin to grow dry and rigid, leaving us increasingly intolerant of the new. We can become one-sided people.

One of the difficulties common to all is that the general growth of consciousness has brought with it over the years its own problems and has placed us in opposition to our instincts, which connect us to nature. Most of us suffer because we cling on the one hand to the childhood level of consciousness and on the other hand we resist all the forces around us that would involve us in the new world, rejecting everything strange and indulging only our own pleasure and powers. Neurotic people become ill because they are unconscious of their problems. Normal people suffer from their conscious problems but without becoming ill.

The demands of life put an end to the idealistic dreams that we had in adolescence. False assumptions give us our first experience of conscious problems. Sometimes this experience is the upset of our psychic equilibrium through our sexual instincts – or from deep feelings of insecurity and unbearable sensitivity in spite of outward and material success. Either we seem to estrange ourselves from the past by identifying with the new, or we estrange ourselves from the new by identifying with the past. In either case we reinforce the narrowness of our individual consciousness instead of shattering it in the tension of the opposites and building up a state of higher and wider consciousness. If we merely limit ourselves to the obvious and attainable, we renounce at the same time all our psychic potentialities. The important lesson we must all learn is that the meaning and purpose of the difficulties that life sets us does not lie in their solution but in the working on them incessantly; otherwise we become fixed and cramped into a narrow mould and are finally stultified spiritually.

Everything that we should and yet cannot be lives on as unconscious contents which can project themselves onto incongruous objects. Anything that throws light onto the darkness of unconscious contents enlarges consciousness. Primitive and irrational fears of the dark go back to primaeval time. We have all experienced a certain kind of distress when dealing with very negative people who fail to see that which appears to be so clear to all those friends around them. They seem to be quite in the dark about those things that appear to be so very clear to us.

We live in a constant pendulum swing between contending forces of all kinds, and this is seen not only in the pairs of opposite spheres on the Tree, but in the vertical relationship of those spheres, the two side pillars of the Tree: the Pillar of Mercy or force, with Chokmah its root, and the Pillar of Severity of form, with its root in Binah. (See lower diagram on pae 106.)

It is within the constant counter-pull between these pillars that we must find our way in life. That way is represented by the central Pillar of Equilibrium, and when we ourselves hold to the consciousness of Tiphareth at the centre of the pillar, we are open to full experience of that way – complete presence in total harmony and balance in all we are and do, directly connected with the greatest depths of the unconscious.

This experiencing is symbolized for us in one of the cards of the Tarot (which itself represents an aspect of the Tree of Life). Isis, the High Priestess, is associated with the central pillar of Mildness or Equilibrium and stands for the equilibrating power between the right-hand column of mercy and initiative, and the left-hand column of severity and resistance – between the 'yes' and the 'no.'

In Chinese philosophy Isis corresponds to the Tao, and the right-hand column to the Yang (or the male primal principle) and the left-hand column to the Yin (or the female primal principle). The three columns or pillars can also be seen as the three channels or 'prana' described by the yogis. The priestess is then Shushumna, the right-hand or masculine is Ida, and the left-hand or feminine, Pingala. In Jungian terms Isis is the whole stream of consciousness itself, both universal and personal.

Isis is the High Priestess of the Inner Temple and she is robed in blue to indicate her heavenly or spiritual nature. The moon in her crown, shimmering on the water swirling around her feet and the base of the columns on either side of her, portrays the cosmic or spiritual element of the Creative World she represents. She is linked to earth by the cube on which she sits. This cube is Malkuth, or what has actually occurred or what *actually* exists. She herself expresses the very real presence of that which was, is, and ever shall be - the river of Confucius 'that flows on and on, without pause, day and night'. She is the immutable, eternal law at work in all change, the course of things, Tao, the one in the many. We say, 'let things take their course,' meaning, let things happen as they will without any interference. In other words, this world is like the flow of water. Do not try to grasp it; you cannot. Time is a form of this movement but the life force is timeless and not static. There is no dissociation between this eternal life and our world of Malkuth. They are like colour and shape, the two combined together are beautiful and harmonious.

To become free of time is to begin to make good use out of it. To be involved in it is to be trapped and imprisoned and never to have enough time to do anything. We have to learn to live eternal life in the fixed world of time and form. Then we become living examples of this spirit and not merely mechanical models. The Chinese say Tao does nothing so nothing is left undone. The High Priestess is the feminine and receptive aspect of this wonderful, miraculous life power. She is known to Hindu philosophy as Prakriti; she is the unifying intelligence and the connecting medium which, in the sense of our relationships with one another, can only happen at a deeper level. When we meet one another through her we call it rapport and recognition.

The all-pervading life-power is recorded as natural law in the collective and cosmic unconsciousness. The scroll that lies on Isis' lap, the Torah, is the record of all those mental and physical states indelibly impressed in the unconscious.

The unconscious is an extremely fluid state. It is everything of which we know but are not at the moment thinking, everything of which we were conscious but have now forgotten, everything perceived by our senses but not noted by our conscious mind. It is all the future things that are taking shape in us and that will some time come into consciousness. The interplay of the conscious and unconscious is of alternating shades of light and darkness. Inner equilibrium is the result of the balance of these contending forces, which consequently must pull one against the other. In the symbol of the I Ching we have a perfect expression of this play of light and dark, masculine and feminine, positive and negative, in which as the one waxes the other wanes and each contains the seed of the other. The creative is masculine; the receptive is feminine and form-making. Only the right complementary harmony can unite the two together in a fruitful way. The equal-armed cross on the breast of Isis the High Priestess shows this union of active (upright) and passive (horizontal) or masculine and feminine elements. According to Greek mythology, Hecate, patroness of all crossroads, was represented by the equal armed cross. But perfect equilibrium would be a complete state of rest, and only through the upset of this equilibrium can the forces again be freed for action and change, growth and evolution to take place.

There is all the difference in the world between the swinging of a pendulum and the tight grip of a vice or a clamp. In poise there must always be a slight vibration, a movement between the opposing forces that hold it steady. Any resistance against which we have to strain in life is not evil but a necessary counterpoise of whatever force we are employing. Unless the two function together, one will run to excess, destroying all balance. We must realise that if we give way to one-sided force in us, it is powerful destructive force that we release. We very soon find that we are not only expressing the impulses of our own shadow side and undeveloped nature but eventually become carried away by a force greater than ourselves, by which we can become swept away to self-destruction. Whenever we open ourselves as a channel to any pure force whether destructive or constructive we open ourselves to a veritable river of energy. It is vitally necessary to become conscious of this so that it can become directed creatively.

The inherent nature of the spirit consists in the eternal inter-action of love and beauty as the active and passive polarity of being. Love is the prime moving power of the creative spirit, but form is necessary to give it perfect expression. It is only when the veil behind Isis, the High Priestess, is penetrated by conscious impulses on our part that the creative activity of the unconscious can be realised and given outward form.

This dualism of the opposites either ends by widening our horizon in spite of our resistances, or we protect ourselves to such a degree from any increase of consciousness that we end by regressing backwards into a neurosis.

What can we learn from the mystics? The mystic tends always towards a state of being in which this duality of human existence is unified in God. It is a dynamic and living impulse through which there is a transformation of the personality. The Christian calls it 'putting on the New Man. Not only is there a change of values but a complete change in intellectual, emotional, and instinctive habits. The minute we open ourselves to the channel of positive light forces, we become 'mystically' intuitive. Delacroix wrote, 'Mystical intuition is not consciousness in the sense of a series of logical implications drawn from sensible representation, neither is it sentiment if we take that word "mystical" to mean the consciousness of organic conditions. In fact, it partakes of both but transcends any mental attitude we may have and is essentially spontaneous. By this I mean that it is received passively by the subject who then begins very gradually to develop all the mystical potentialities of the unconscious. You might see it as a kind of spiritual maturing which starts to take place within. Suddenly the characteristic features of this hidden activity begin bursting into consciousness as unexpected revelations.'

Most of us find that contemplation and action tend to be enemies. It is necessary to find a synthesis as both contemplation and action are important. Contemplation tends to destroy action by its distracting influence, while action in its turn is inhibited by contemplation. But when action springs from contemplation itself, we know it is God acting from within. We are no longer under the delusion that we are the doer of the actions, but know that He is. Heinrich Suso, the 14th century priest-mystic and follower of Eckhart, said, 'In such a man, God is the essence, the life and the operation, and the man is no more than his instrument.'

10

THE POLES

The most important spheres in the structure of the Tree are its poles, Kether and Malkuth, the extremes of the central pillar which is the axis of the cosmos. It is around their interrelating that the whole cosmos functions and the other spheres find their place. Without it, a flood of uncontrolled life-force would bring disintegration and the cosmos would filter away into chaos. All the lesser relationships and combinations of spheres are contained within this greater one, which consists in Spirit expressing itself eternally and perfectly in Matter, and perfect Matter transforming itself ceaselessly back into Spirit. This is the expansion and contraction, the vast breathing-out and breathing-in that is the life-breath of cosmic evolution. And at its centre is the still place where human consciousness can know full awareness of the wondrous and essential rhythm and harmony of all things.

*

St Gregory once said a very profound thing: 'We cannot see the visible, except with the invisible.' The whole mystery of life is in this extraordinary relationship between what appears to be very small and limited, and the limitless, the fathomless.

In the same way that the invisible 'sees' the visible, so does the quiet, passive watchfulness and silent attention of the small and limited reveal the limitless. This is not speculation but a fact to be tried and tested. To be – is to *be* in relationship, the relationship of the limited to the limitless. This relationship is Life – and the beginning of the ending, and the ending of the beginning. Only in this mirror of relationship can we even begin to see ourselves clearly. I must begin and end with I AM – with what I AM and who I AM. There was a famous Sanyasin (a wandering Buddhist ascetic) who searched the whole world for Truth, going from one famous Teacher to another only to find when he returned sad and disillusioned that this precious jewel was in his own home.

At its source in the individual, the river of consciousness is so small it is hardly worth noticing. But as it opens up and gathers momentum, it flows forward powerfully to blend with the eternal, timeless and unknown ocean of truth. It is this Truth alone that frees our poor, limited mind from its own imprisonment, its own bondage. This bondage is made up of memory, distracting thoughts, fixed ideas, prejudices and conditioning, all of which are obstacles to that which is not of time. Mind, conditioned mind, is the creator of time and the user of time. All thinking is in time. Without thought, time is non-existent. Thought, accumulated knowledge, the storing of memory, effort and will are limited in time and are of time. Can we, through the attention of the heart, through stillness and passive watchfulness, break through the barrier of Time created by our own thinking, into the limitless and the unknown?

When one is completely passive, watchful and in a state of stillness, one can see all things going through the cycle of changes and returning to their original state. Things grow and develop in various ways but they all return to the common source. This returning to the source is what is meant by the state of stillness, and that stillness means that things have reached their appointed end. Everything, however small and apparently insignificant, matters when we realize that we cannot discount anything at all until the awareness, having grown complete, becomes enlightenment. Similarly, in an opposite direction it is the accumulations of many small wrongs thoughtlessly done which create weakness and turmoil in us. We can only help others from our own strength and that lies in understanding ourselves first.

This does not mean that we must identify with our egotistic self, labelling it 'good' or 'bad,' 'intelligent' or 'foolish,' 'a success' or 'a failure.' What it does mean is that instead we must see this little self as an illusory reflection of our true Self, to recognise that I AM rather than identifying all the time with the illusory, the unreal, and the transitory. We can only enter this depth, this I AM, through the door of the heart centre. To do this we have to be emptied of all the burdens and accumulations of the mind, leaving this clutter behind in the superficial, illusory, surface world to which it belongs. Only by this complete abandonment and surrender, which in itself releases a tremendous, attentive, one-pointed energy, can we discover and come face to face with Truth. Love is total abandonment without fear or desire. So long as we cling to false securities and habits and to dependency on others, we cannot be free from pain or free to love. The first step is self-knowledge, not through any one else but by being aware of our own behaviour, our everyday relationships and our thoughts without condemnation or justification. This is a process of constant discovery in the fullness of living each moment totally and not partially.

There can be goodness and generosity only when the mind is quiet. Beauty (Tiphareth), that something which is really God, comes into being only when there is complete abandonment of the self. This is what is meant by self-surrender. Our resistance to this tells us that our hearts are not in what we are doing, so we start inventing motives for what we do. Looking and observing without resistance is surrender. Attention without personal motive is love.

In complete attention and total surrender, there must be no sense of condemnation or comparison of that which you discover. Look at your self in the mirror of relationship without judging what you see. Out of this depth of self-knowledge comes time-lessness and the experience of love. If we know how to live, then living itself is Truth. However we have lost the beauty of living richly, worshipping each day with abundance, neither looking back nor forward to tomorrow. This is the eternal present, the here and the now. Trying to become something, we miss this tense, abundant love of the Now, this living in depth and fullness. When you are listening to everything in life, and watching yourself in the mirror of relationship from moment to moment, then it is that the mind is really still. In that stillness and full attention, that which cannot be described or speculated upon comes into being. Our mind is so restless, afraid to be still, yet out of that very stillness wisdom comes. A mind full of conflict and intellectual knowledge is a mind full of misery. Wisdom can only come to the still mind, the mind that is silent, alert and passive. Because of loneliness, we desire to be loved; because of loneliness we turn on the T.V., the radio, go to the cinema or seek other forms of distraction. We want to run away, to escape from our loneliness. Yet if we can dare to be still and stand and look at this emptiness, then we find we are capable of being alone – not lonely, but alone, which is our true individuality. In this aloneness Reality is possible – it is possible to BE – and to perceive Truth, that which is God. Then the mind that is empty like the begging bowl is able to receive that which is Eternal.

A story: The Three Pillars and The Tree

In the Middle Ages the Tree of Adam became the Tree of the Cross. Among the legends of Adam's later years is one which has been handed down in many forms. It tells how Adam, exhausted after uprooting a huge bush, sent forth Seth to beg of the Angel who guarded the entrance of Paradise, some of the ambrosia from the Divine tree so that he might rub it on his limbs and regain health and strength.

As Seth approached the Tree with the Angel, he saw seated in it a radiant youth, who told him he was the Son of God, and that he would one day come to earth to deliver it from sin, and, when he did so, he would give the Oil of Mercy to Adam. The Guardian Angel then gave three small seeds to Seth, and told him to place them beneath his father's tongue when he should bury him near Mount Tabor. This Seth did, and in a little while the three seeds appeared above the earth as three wands; one of olive, the second of cedar, and the third of cypress.

The three saplings remained growing from the mouth of Adam, but they were not recognised until the time of Moses, who was told by God in a vision to cut them. He did so, and with the three wands performed many miracles. After the death of Moses the wands lay concealed in the valley of Hebron until the time of King David who, bidden by the Holy Ghost, found them and took them to Jerusalem, where the sick and lame of the city beseeched him to grant them the salvation of the Cross. On being touched by the holy wands they were instantly cured of their ills. David was then said to have put the three saplings into a cistern, and, on going to them the next day, found that they had taken root and had become bound up together, so that the three grew as one and put forth a single stem, that of the cedar. The cedar was placed in the Temple where, after a long period, it was cut down by Solomon.

A woman who saw the sacred trunk lying with other timber to be used for the completion of the Temple, lay down on it and, filled with the spirit of prophesy, cried aloud, 'Now the Lord God predicts the virtue of the Holy Cross.' The Jews attacked the woman and threw the sacred wood into the piscina probatica, whose water at once acquired healing properties and was called the Pool of Bethesda. In the hope of profaning it, the Jews next used the wood in the construction of a bridge, over which the people passed, unconscious of its holy nature. But the Queen of Sheba threw herself down upon it and prophesied that the Cross of the Saviour of mankind would be made from the wood.

Thus as Folkard remarks, although Adam, by eating of the Tree of Knowledge deprived himself of the fruit of the Tree of Life, yet from his mouth sprang the tree whose wood supplied the Cross of Christ, by means of which the race of Adam attained everlasting life.

HISTORIES AND DIAGRAMS

HISTORY OF THE TREE OF LIFE

The belief that the world was born of a Vast Tree, and that man is descended from it, has been held by humanity from the earliest religious times. It is found in old Norse tales, as well as in the traditions of ancient China, Japan and India. The concept probably came to the eastern Mediterranean with the migration of the Indo-European peoples, some 15,000 years BC.

According to another tradition the ancient Hebrew Tree of Life originated with Abraham, believed to have lived circa 2300 BC. He is the patriarch to whom not only the Jewish people but many Arabic tribes trace their ancestry. Arab legend states that he laid the foundation of the sanctuary at Mecca. Greek legend remembers him as King of Damascus. Hebrew legend refers to him as the repository of all wisdom and science, and prototype of humility and kindness.

Abraham was born into a world overrun by the Babylonian and Egyptian civilizations. Living the nomadic life, in mature years he searched contemporary religions, and on meeting Melchizedek, the Priest-King of Salem (Jerusalem) was initiated by him into the highest knowledge. Following this, and after a visit to Egypt, Abraham is said to have concluded the monotheistic principle – that all gods are but one God.

The importance of Judaism in the history of religion is that it was the first to adopt this principle, and monotheism is its main legacy to both Christianity and Islam. The Tree of Life teaching is essentially an explanation of 'the many which are One.'

Legend also tells that a thousand years later, when Moses received on Mount Sinai the written law of the Commandments, he was also given instruction about the Tree, with a taboo on its transmission other than orally.

The Tree of Life was certainly being taught by rabbis around 515 BC, and scholars maintain that sound knowledge of it is clearly evidenced in the words, behaviour and whole outlook of Christ himself.

There was much interchange of knowledge between wise men of different nations and traditions during the few hundred years before Christ, which may have led to the abandonment of the oral rule and the writing in the 1st century AD of the earliest known book about the Tree – The Book of Formation, or *Sepher Yetzirah*. Its publication, together with the dispersion of the Jews in the next century, took the teaching all over Europe and beyond, and its knowledge and understanding were influenced by Persian, Greek and eventually Arabian thought, and by Gnosticism and Neoplatonism.

Different schools were devoted to teaching it in Provence in the 12th century, and the first known mention of the name Qabalah appeared there in the 13th century. Spain then became its main centre, with schools in several cities, and it was here that the knowledge flowered in The Book of Splendour, or *Zohar*, a great compendium of writings by Moses de Leon, who died in 1305. From it, all later teaching of the Tree derives.

The Tree was well known to scholars in Renaissance Italy and by the early 17th century it was studied and discussed at the Medici court by its most brilliant minds. In the 17th and 18th centuries it also flourished in Poland and Russia (where whole communities lived by it) and from Spain it spread to North Africa and the Turkish empire. In the 19th century in Britain it was taken up as a mystery tradition by various semi-religious groups, and it is their work, continuing on into the 20th century, which has given rise to ever widening use here of the Tree as a system of knowledge, understanding and development.

HISTORY OF THE MONDAY GROUP

In 1957 Buntie Wills took over the guidance of a study group of which she herself was a member. This 'Monday Group' had previously been led since its inception in 1937 by Buntie's teacher, Toni Sussman, who was also a psychotherapist and a former pupil of Carl Jung.

Concerned to carry out to the utmost of her ability the task she had accepted, Buntie asked another member, Helah Fox, to offer her knowledge as well, and so developed a whole new pattern of working for the group. Helah had studied the Tree of Life extensively with Dion Fortune.

The group's membership was a changing entity. There were about 14 members at any one time, but occasionally someone left and someone new was invited by Buntie and the group to take their place. In this way about 24 people were involved during the years when Buntie led it. It was a rule that all who joined must be or have been in therapy.

Each year there was a programme of work with an overall title, and the meetings averaged 13 a year, divided into three terms. The group met in a little waiting room upstairs at 10a Cunningham Place, where Buntie lived and worked. Each meeting began with a meditation on the Tree conducted by

Helah Fox, followed by discussion of the evening's subject related to it. After a coffee break, Buntie gave a talk developing the subject in Jungian terms. She would never talk without notes because she was concerned that whatever she said was exactly right. Instead, she took great time and trouble to write her talks fully beforehand, each usually some two thousand words long.

In this way she wrote for the group more than 140 talks, and in doing so she left her teaching and understanding 'formed and shaped' on paper – distilled out of her work and experience, as well as from her own spiritual growth during those years.

Many who were in therapy with Buntie will remember her explaining some matter or other to them in terms of the geometric patterns of the Tree of Life. In her own words, 'It is the key to all religious systems, and the great art of secret or hidden relationship.' She regarded it as a fine instrument for spiritual development.

Programmes of the group's work included: The Natural World; The Qabalah itself; The Tarot (related to the Tree); Paths of Spiritual Growth; The Family; The Way, the Truth and the Life; The Cell and the Body and their relationship to the Soul and the Universe; Communication; The Senses; The Inner Landscape; Guilt and Redemption; and Fairy Tales.

For fourteen years Buntie led all this work. There was a time when she was seriously ill and only managed to put together a few rough notes for meetings; the members learned then how to take up responsibility for their meeting themselves. One member became terminally ill, and all lived through a long experiencing of that illness and the passing which followed it. Another member had to live abroad for a good spell, and ways were found to keep him in active touch with the work. Sometimes studies were too arduous, or perplexing, and everyone learned to lighten them with humour. At times there were stresses in the group, and people found their way to creating something out of them. Eventually change itself brought the group to an end and everyone quietly moved out of it into their own individual paths, while Buntie turned her energies to the wider and more numerous groups that followed it in Studio E.

WORKING DIAGRAMS

THE TRIADS and THE PILLARS

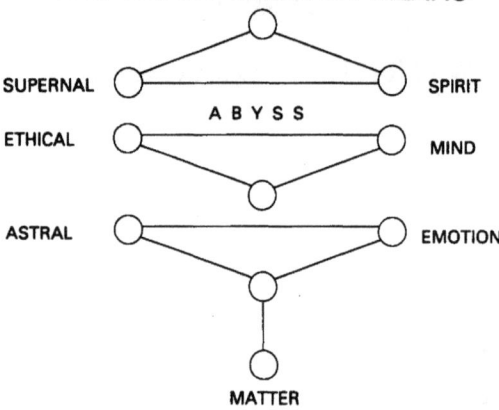

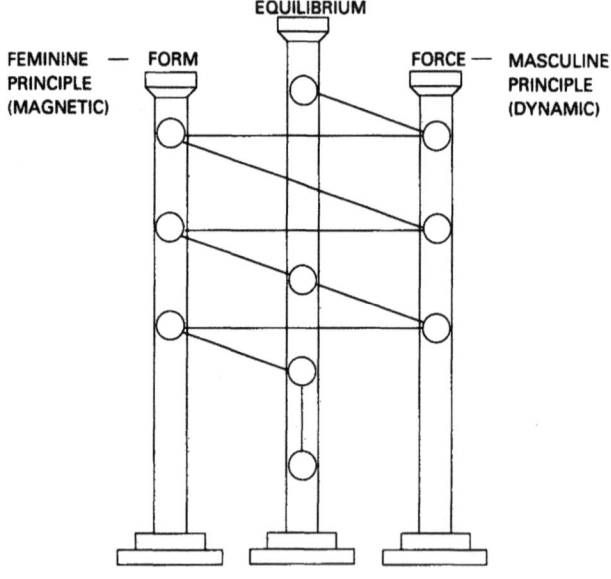

THE TREE OF LIFE

- THE CROWN — Kether
- UNDERSTANDING — Binah
- WISDOM — Chokmah
- SEVERITY — Geburah
- MERCY — Chesed
- BEAUTY — Tiphareth
- SPLENDOUR — Hod
- VICTORY — Netzach
- THE FOUNDATION — Yesod
- THE KINGDOM — Malkuth

www.ingramcontent.com/pod-product-compliance
Lightning Source LLC
Chambersburg PA
CBHW060202050426
42446CB00013B/2946